THE DAVID B. NELLUM STORY

VINDICATED

Healing from the Shame of Boyhood

Sexual Abuse Through Christ

DAVID B. NELLUM

Foreword By Rev. Dr. Candace Kelly

The David B. Nellum Story

Vindicated: Healing from the Shame of Boyhood Sexual Abuse Through Christ
by David B. Nellum

Printed and bound in the United States of America

Published by Cole Publishing

Library of Congress
Cataloging-in-Publication Data
ISBN: 979-8-9885825-5-7

Cole Publishing
4067 Hardwick Street #282
Lakewood, CA 90712

Email: ccpprod@aol.com
Book Cover Design by Covenant Images
For Book Orders:
Contact us at Cole Publishing Company

Cole Publishing

CONTENTS

AUTHOR'S NOTE

This book follows a conversation over several months with a trusted pastor and mentor. I have chosen to keep the interview format to better capture the life-giving back-and-forth process of sharing our stories and encourage those who may find themselves somewhere along a similar journey. You too can see healing and victory!

All names, except my own and that of my pastor, have been changed to protect the privacy of those involved.

DEDICATION

I dedicate this healing endeavor to the memories of my Mother and Father, Maple Nellum and Joseph Alexander. Thank you, Mom, for doing and being your best through your own healing. Thank you, Dad; I treasure the final years that we had together.

- To my spiritual Dads: Apostle Robbie Horton, thank you for teaching me the principles and foundation of prayer.

- Pastor James C. Kelly, your faithful encouragement and exhortations always served to lift me and compel me forward in the things of God. Thank you for providing Diane and me with sound biblical premarital counseling and walking before us as a faithful husband, pastor and friend.

- Both of my spiritual Dad's contributions were instrumental in shaping me into the man that I am today. Your memories will remain in my heart always.

This book is also dedicated to all the young boys whose experiences have left them feeling voiceless, not good enough, abandoned, ashamed, and without hope; who have been violated physically, emotionally, and spiritually. Please know that there is a path to the other side of your pain - a path to hope and fulfillment. Your journeys are not in vain.

ACKNOWLEDGMENTS

I want to thank my Lord and Savior Jesus Christ for saving my soul by bringing me out of darkness into His marvelous light. I also want to thank my Heavenly Father for charging me to write this book as a source of my inner healing, and also as a testimony for many who will pick it up.

There are some things in life that you cannot do on your own, and God will send the perfect vessel to accompany you, as He did with Deborah and Barak. To this end, I want to acknowledge my Pastor, Rev. Dr. Candace Kelly, who is also my spiritual Mom, for escorting me through the birthing process to draw this book out of me, and for walking me through the steps of healing, helping me to forgive the hurts I didn't deserve. Thank you for the transformative process that unveiled the greater me that has longed to be vindicated! The years, months, weeks, days and hours spent working on this manuscript together was worth it! My gratitude to the staff at Cole Publishing Company for your extraordinary professionalism.

With sincere gratitude and appreciation, I want to acknowledge those who have been present with me during the various seasons of my journey, who encouraged and supported me, whose love has uplifted me, and whose foundation has helped shape me. I'm doing my best to include those near and dear to me; for anyone that I may overlook, please charge it to my head and not my heart as there are so many to name. You are loved.

- A special thank you to my lovely wife of 14 years, Diane Nellum: you have been a blessing from God, my inspiration and my motivation. I would not be the man I am today without your love, support and confidence in me. Your kindness, your thoughtfulness, your tenderness and patience is a gift. I understand now what it means when the scripture declares, "when a man finds a wife, he finds a good thing and favor with the Lord." You are my good thing!

- My sisters, Kattie and Diann, you never stopped praying for me, even when I didn't want to hear it. Thank you for your perseverance for my soul.

- My brother, Sammy Joe, as well as my gone-too-soon brothers Lee and Bryant, I will love you forever.

- Shelley, I am thankful for you and our four beautiful children. Your commitment to parenting in my absence is a testament to your dedication to motherhood.

- To my daughters, Paradise and Davshavou, you are queens. To my sons, David Jr. and Davion, you are kings and what a privilege it is to be your Dad. I am super proud of each of you.

- To my grandchildren A'Journey, Davion Jr, and A'Dryeam, I am grateful to be your Paw Paw; and I am anxiously awaiting the arrival of David III. In loving memory of my grandsons Lyyric and Kam'ron, you will never be forgotten.

- To my Mother-in-Law, Dorothy Moss. Thank you, Mom, for your love, support and wisdom. It has been a blessing to have you around. You are like a breath of fresh air. Thank you for the joy your laughter creates.

- My PHAZE 3 brothers: Bill McCormick and Derek Newman (RIP Rodney McCormick, Sr.), I am grateful for all the lessons we learned along the way and for how you welcomed me into the group and taught me how to harmonize.

- To my DDT brothers: DeFrantz Forrest and Tony Davis, what great music we have created together.

- Ms. Lee, my elementary school teacher: thank you for seeing value in me when others could not or would not.

- Florence Abram, who gave me refuge on so many occasions during my childhood.

- Nashon Abram, my childhood best friend who I treasure.

- Pastor Rene and Rev Melrose: thank you for modeling godliness, commitment, and dedication to marriage.

- Anthony and Rev. Melissa Tucker: thank you for your friendship over the years.

- Terry Nicholson (the songbird), thank you for your passion and boldness in Christ. Your one flesh, the late and great Deacon Micheal Nicholson, will forever be in my heart!

- Kenny and Daciena Green: I am grateful for our partnership in Global Ministry spreading the Good News of Jesus Christ. Your friendship is deeply appreciated.

- Apostle Vicki Lee: I am grateful for your birthing ministry that has blessed my life.

- Pastor Larry Alexander: thank you for your godly encouragement and guidance.

- Haskel Jackson, my brother: thank you for your creative innovations, and for sharing your talents with me and pushing me as an artist.

- My Acts Community Bible Church family, including the Men of Integrity: we are better together!

FOREWORD

Rev. Dr. Candace Kelly

Research by the Centers for Disease Control and Prevention[1] has shown that one in five Americans was sexually molested as a child, one in four was beaten by a parent to the point of a mark being left on their body, and one in three couples engages in physical violence. Many of us grew up with alcoholic relatives, and one out of eight witnessed their mother being beaten or hit.

To our shock time and time again, traumatic experiences leave indelible traces, whether on a huge scale, or on our families with dark secrets being imperceptibly passed down through generations. They also leave traces on our minds and emotions, on our capacity for joy and intimacy, and even on our biology and immune systems. We often underestimate the physiological impact that sexual abuse has on the human life.

In his book, *The Body Keeps The Score*, Bessel Van Der Kolk, M.D. explains that it is common for the victim of sexual trauma to want to move on and move beyond the trauma; but the part of our brain that is devoted to ensuring our survival (deep below our rational brain) is not very good at denial. Long after a traumatic experience is over, it may be reactivated at the slightest hint of danger and mobilize disturbed brain circuits, secreting massive amounts of stress hormones. This precipitates unpleasant emotions, intense physical sensations, and impulsive and aggressive actions. These posttraumatic reactions feel incomprehensible and overwhelming. Feeling out of control, survivors of trauma often begin to fear that they are damaged to the core and beyond redemption.

In the face of trauma, the journey to healing and restoration is seldom linear. It is a path fraught with emotional upheaval, profound self-discovery, and the tireless pursuit of justice. *Vindicated*, by David Nellum, is not merely a recounting of events, but a powerful testament to the resilience of the human spirit in the aftermath of sexual assault.

---

1 V.Felitti, et al. "Relationships of Childhood Abuse and Household Dysfunction to Many of the Leading Causes of Death in Adults: The Adverse Childhood Experiences (ACE) Study." American Journal of Prevention Medicine 14, no.4 (1998):245-58.

This book is a courageous narrative that delves deep into the complexities of recovery, the quest for vindication, and the ultimate triumph of the truth.

David Nellum's story is one of profound bravery. His candid exploration of his experiences invites readers to witness the raw and often painful realities of surviving sexual assault. Through his eyes, we see not only the immediate impacts of such trauma but also the long-term effects on one's psyche and relationships. Nellum's narrative does not shy away from the harsh truths; instead, it embraces them, providing a beacon of hope for others who find themselves in similar battles.

What sets *Vindicated* apart is its unwavering focus on the themes of healing and restoration. Nellum offers an honest portrayal of the arduous journey toward emotional and psychological recovery. His reflections are imbued with a sense of authenticity that only someone who has walked this path can convey. His story is a reminder that healing is possible, even in the face of the deepest wounds, and that restoration, while challenging, is within reach.

The pursuit of vindication is another crucial element of this book. Nellum's determination to seek justice and clear his name underscores the importance of standing up against injustice. His perseverance in the face of overwhelming odds is both inspiring and empowering. It serves as a powerful reminder that one's voice can be a formidable tool in the fight for truth and justice.

Vindicated is more than a memoir; it is a call to action. It urges us to listen, to believe, and to support survivors of sexual assault. It challenges societal stigmas and encourages a deeper understanding of the complexities surrounding such experiences. David Nellum's story is a crucial contribution to the ongoing conversation about sexual assault, offering insights that are both enlightening and transformative.

As you turn the pages of this book, prepare to be moved by Nellum's honesty, strength, and resilience. *Vindicated* is a testament to the human capacity for healing and the unyielding pursuit of justice. It is a story of triumph!

This book is a vital contribution to the ongoing conversation about sexual assault and the long, often painful road to recovery. It stands as a testament to the fact that, through courage and solidarity, we can create a world where justice prevails and survivors are truly vindicated. May *Vindicated* offer solace to those who need it, understanding to those who seek it, and a clarion call to all who read it: that healing, restoration, and justice are not just possible, but inevitable, with perseverance and hope.

CHAPTER 1

Stability

PASTOR CK: David, I am honored to journey with you on this self-exploration of healing through storytelling. I believe God has a real blessing for you at the end of this journey to His Glory and to His honor.

DAVID: I want to say thank you for taking this assignment, Pastor. I must admit--- I am nervous and don't know what to expect, but I am trusting you and God in this long overdue process. I am also grateful for my older siblings, whom I could call the family historians, who passed down much of the story I will share here. I know this is a unique way to write my book, but I am glad I have your support, prayers and guidance.

PASTOR CK: Ok. Let's get started, shall we? David, can you tell me, what is your primary reason for writing your autobiography?

DAVID: I believe God wants to reveal to other men, and young boys in particular, that no matter what they have gone through in this broken world, He is their Vindicator. What the Devil meant for their destruction, God can turn into good.

PASTOR CK: Alright, where shall we start?

DAVID: There is something that has unsettled me deeply for years that I want to explore. Growing up, we were moving all the time, and I never really felt planted and anchored. It seemed like every six or seven years, we were headed to a new destination. Examining this part of my journey revealed to me how hard it was to feel a sense of stability and home. I think I craved that without even knowing it. As a young boy, I was not old enough to voice those feelings of frustration or understand the psychosocial issues my mother was having until later.

PASTOR CK: I hear you saying that moving around caused you a sense of instability which resulted in feelings of insecurity.

DAVID: Exactly—never knowing how long this would be my home. Then there were times we had to live with other people who helped my mother out. Let me chronicle that part of my journey...

The First House

The first house we lived in when I was born, according to my sister, was 52nd Street off Compton Ave. We were there from 1962-1969.

We lived there until I was six or seven years of age. A deep sadness often comes upon me when I reflect on this house.

PASTOR CK: If you can remember, tell me what this sadness is related to?

DAVID: I believe it is because I have no memory of my mom at that address. That's the sad part. It feels strange. I can see everybody but her. I don't see her, and it frustrates me and sometimes her absence scares me.

My sister Kathryn helped me with this part of my recollection, saying, "she was never there." Kathryn explained that she would pick me up from school at 3pm, and then leave me with Kathryn or my other sister, Daisy, while she went to hang out with her best friend and drinking buddy, Aunt Ruthie. I could not understand why she did not want to spend time with her children. I would cry for her. I still remember that today.

PASTOR CK: That saddens me, David. I can see that it is still very raw for you. Did you feel abandoned?

DAVID: Yes, because I thought, "If she loved me, she would want to be with me and be there for me when I wake up and go to sleep and hear about my day when I got home from school." But she chose her friends over me. It used to anger me. I felt abandoned. This feeling of abandonment has been part of almost every intimate relationship that I have ever had. It left a mark on me.

I just wanted a normal mom... a sober mom who smelled like orange juice and not alcohol. I wanted to know her and for her to know me. I always thought to myself,

"If she stays sober, then we can have a regular conversation like other kids have with their moms."

If she had stayed home more, she would have been there when I got home from school. Then, I would have been able to tell her all about my day and what happened to me in school. I really wanted her to be there! I wanted her to be my loving and caring mother, but she missed a lot of what happened to me. If she had stayed sober then maybe she could have appreciated me more as her son, as someone she could have loved, and perhaps I could have loved her more. I often think - if only we had had that quality time together. When she was leaving us, I would run to the door begging her to stay home. I would cry, but I could not get her to stay. She obviously wanted whatever was beyond those doors more than what she was leaving at home.

There were times I just felt invisible, as if she could not see me, and I did not matter to her. If she would have just hugged me and told me how much she loved me – but she did not. I know I was not the only sibling to feel this way, but I can only feel my personal pain. I hope someday, God will heal my heart from these ghosts as well.

PASTOR CK: I believe that is certainly His purpose and promise. You are bringing these cares to Him because you know He cares for you.

DAVID: This may sound strange for a four- or five-year-old, but I was a wanderer. I would walk away from home without anyone really noticing. As a young boy, I remember feeling that nobody cared where I was.

One day, I was almost kidnapped. I was about five years old and walking to the candy store. As I was passing by the church on the corner of 52nd and Compton, this black car pulled up quickly and a tall black man jumped out. He grabbed me, and I was able to pull away and wiggle out of his grip.

I remember running as fast as I could. I ran to a neighbor's house that lived in front of us. The husband opened the door and after I told him what happened, he called the police. They came quickly and took me to the police station.

PASTOR CK: Tell me this was your last time roaming the streets all by yourself.

DAVID: I wish I could, but I remember getting lost on several occasions. And you are not going to believe this, but I drove through that same block today.

PASTOR CK: How did you feel? What was that like?

DAVID: It was eerie... I had a feeling of emptiness and sadness, because it reminded me of feeling left out and longing for my mom.

PASTOR CK: Those feelings are very powerful, right?

DAVID: Yes. I cannot believe I am still experiencing these raw feelings as if it was yesterday.

PASTOR CK: You know they say in grief psychology that anything we have not processed will stay buried inside of us until we address the pain, the brokenness and the unforgiveness.

DAVID: I guess I am a living witness that I have not dealt with these things in their fullness.

PASTOR CK: David, part of your childhood was a loss. You must grieve the loss of the maternal relationship you always longed for and never quite received.

DAVID: Yeah, I guess I do.

CHAPTER 2

Forgiveness

PASTOR CK: Have you forgiven your mother for abandoning you as a boy?

DAVID: Let me answer it in this way: I remember one evening when I was living with my mom as an adult. I asked her to sit down and have a talk with me. I needed to get some things off my chest concerning my childhood. My mother agreed and made me feel comfortable enough to share what I have been holding on to all these years. I began sharing how hurt I was as a little boy without my mother. I do not think she was prepared for all I had to say, but she was open and never interrupted me. She listened with her heart, which made it easy for me. It got intense as I described my needs as a boy.

I told her about some of my deepest secrets that I could not tell anybody. She was nowhere around to protect me. My voice elevated, and I know my face showed how angry I was, but she sat there bullet-proof; almost like she knew I had to get it all out of me. That day, I told her I forgave her, not realizing that forgiveness is layered; and while my heart intended to forgive her fully, the pain went deeper than I even knew. I did not know this was only level one of releasing.

My mom sat there watching her grown son revert to the ages I needed her the most. Each age had to have flashed in her heart; I could see the grimace of pain she felt, but also the strength that God gave her to withstand the blows of truth that no parent wants to hear. As badly as I wanted to tell her, I also did not want to hurt her; but it had to come out for me to experience some kind of resolution and reconciliation with my mom.

PASTOR CK: You felt better once you got it off your chest?

> That was my first dose of His grace-medicine that he applied to me through my mother.

DAVID: Yes, I did. I felt like I was not hiding my feelings from her; like all I needed to say at that point was out and in the open. I just didn't realize it would not happen in one sharing. It simply opened the floodgates to have the opportunity to seep out at times.

PASTOR CK: For anyone getting sober and coming to Christ, it does not erase the trail of consequences you leave behind with your children and those relationships that you hurt during your addiction.

DAVID: Yes. I see that. I wished I could have used a blanket to cover my mom, but I did not have that power. I just had the power to be human and honest. She honored me. She listened to me. She heard me.

PASTOR CK: She loved you. She made it safe for you, David. She mothered you in those moments, just as God does when we come to Him – He does not interrupt us and tell us to grow up, He makes the space welcoming because He knows He will heal us after the painful outburst.

DAVID: Yes, that was my first dose of His grace–medicine that he applied to me through my mother.

PASTOR CK: David, I am glad you can see that the years of anger and resentment are layered. You had almost a lifetime of suppressed emotions resulting in deep rage, and inconsolable grief. You have forgiven her, and you will continuously have to remind yourself when those feelings come that you have settled it with her. How did she respond?

DAVID: I cannot remember every word, but I do remember, "Son, I'm sorry. I cannot tell you how sorry I am that I was not there for you and your siblings. I was a child myself when I think of it, chasing love that didn't want to love me back. Not having the education and skills to take care of all my responsibilities. It was hard. I wanted to give up, but I couldn't. I know you needed my love, my attention, I guess I didn't have it to give then. I do have it to give now if you let me."

PASTOR CK: Did you let her?

DAVID: It was a big step that led us in the right direction. I needed it and she needed it also. I remember crying and rejoicing all at the same time. Crying from the pain, the losses, and regrets, but rejoicing that I have a sober mother in front of me who now is serving God.

But there were still times that I would revert when things would trigger me. That is how I know you are right in saying forgiveness is layered.

PASTOR CK: Sometimes it is about forgiving, letting go, and grieving those things we did not have. In your case, grieving the mom you did not have. When we do not grieve those relational losses, we will transfer those needs into our adult life and require them from our adult intimate relationships. Whatever void that was not filled in a healthy way will be filled in toxic ways.

DAVID: Wow, that's real. If I'm honest, I admit that I can still feel the loss, the longing; I could feel myself wishing my childhood was different and that I had a mom who was there most of the time. While I remember forgiving her, I admit the residue of anger still exists.

PASTOR CK: And when that happens, David, you can continue to own your feelings and name them, and then forgive again. That is normal, because as we said earlier, forgiveness is a process, and especially when it is complex, the layers are unpredictable.

DAVID: I used to fuss at her and out of nowhere remind her that she was not there for us. But the Lord would convict me and say, "If you forgave her, stop throwing it in her face." I guess part of me wanted her to feel the pain that I felt.

PASTOR CK: It sounds like you felt very alone in your pain, right? Maybe you even needed your pain validated.

DAVID: Yes, I can agree with that.

PASTOR CK: Thank God for his Holy Spirit, who wants to heal us and help us. Christ reminds us that he feels everything we feel; we have not a high priest that cannot be touched with the infirmities of our feelings, but in all points tempted such as we were. We must forgive those hurts we did not deserve and receive our Savior's comfort.

DAVID: But she is gone now, how would I keep forgiving her?

PASTOR CK: You can forgive her in your heart. In grief work, we suggest grievers participate in rituals. You are still very much grieving the loss of your mom. There are many rituals you can do: 1) You can write her a letter and read it out loud in front of an empty chair. 2) Some people place their loved one's photo in a chair and verbalize or read the letter to them. 3) Lastly, you can simply verbalize it in a context like this if you are comfortable. Would you like to engage in any of these processes?

DAVID: Yes, I do. I want to share now because I do not want anything in my heart against my mother. I really do not.

PASTOR CK: If she was here, what would you say to her David?

DAVID: Momma, I wish you were there. Every time you would go out those doors, you have no idea how it would crush me. It felt like you loved those streets, your friends, and your parties over me. I needed your affirmation when others would put me down and make fun of me. Life as a little boy was unbearable. I needed your protection when grown people abused me. I was so embarrassed walking around with holes in my shoes and clothes from hand-me-down places. I was humiliated as a young boy, and I did not know where to turn with my pain. You missed my important dates at school, and you were not there when I graduated 6th grade. When they called your name, when I looked out there, you or my father were not there like the other children's parents. Instead of a cheer, the crowd dwindled to a quiet hush. I was so disappointed in you and embarrassed for myself.

So, I walked home by myself that day as if it was just another day. I wanted you to be proud of me on this day, but you were not there. I got my diploma, just cried, and kept it to myself.

You kept leaving. You would not stop. I needed to know that I was good enough and that I was important. I took it personally, believing that you did not want to be around me. I could not read, and I was placed in special education classes. Students and teachers made fun of me and called me "dirty and dumb David." I needed you. I needed you to be there for me so many times. Then the confusion around who my daddy was. It was heartbreaking for me. It hurt me to see my other brothers' and sisters' father come and get them and buy things for them, but I did not have a father who demonstrated his love and care by coming to get me.

I needed the presence of a dad to do what only a father could do for a son trying to grow up in this crazy world. You could not help me with that either. If I had known my real dad early on, and if he was a responsible dad, maybe things would have been different for me. I do not know, but today, I choose to forgive you, Momma. I know now it was your pain, and the choice of alcohol to numb that pain, that kept you from being our momma-- it was not because you did not love us.

So many things were not your fault. You were a victim of the abuse of others, like the man you fell in love with and came to California with, only for him to dump you after meeting somebody else. Today I know what it feels like to be dumped and left by someone you love. Momma, please know that I forgive you, and I am asking God to help me clear my heart of all residues that linger. I ask God to forgive me for being so angry at you. I just didn't understand.

PASTOR CK: What are you feeling?

DAVID: Man, I have never expressed those feelings like that. I feel light - like a load has lifted off me.

PASTOR CK: David, you have made an important step. Forgiveness is a process. Grief is another important process. We must grieve what we have lost. Try not to confuse the two: forgiveness and grief. Sometimes, you could very well just be missing her deeply.

Do not be shocked if something triggers you again. The more you identify those feelings by naming them, you can constructively process and put them where they need to be so that you are not transferring undue emotions to someone else. Where would you like to go from here?

DAVID: Now I would like to share more about my mother's life.

PASTOR CK: I think that is a good transition. It will probably lay some foundation and insight to your mother's choices.

DAVID: Man, you just don't know. She had a rough life, Pastor. It gives me some insight on where I came from.

CHAPTER 3

My Mother's Story
20 Years Earlier

PASTOR CK: Where would you like to start today in sharing part of your mother's journey?

DAVID: My mother, Marie, was born in Belzoni, Mississippi, and had a fourth-grade education. Hers was a difficult journey through this minefield that we call life. My first trip to New Orleans was a real eye-opener! I learned so much about my mother and her family on that vacation, and it explained volumes. I met Auntie Doris and she shared with me a portion of my grandmother's (and in turn, my mother's) history. I learned that my grandfather beat grandma mercilessly. He was an alcoholic who drank night and day.

As I understand it, one day my grandmother got tired of it, and left him and everything she loved behind. She wanted to take my mom, but he threatened her life, telling her that she was not going to take his kids.

My mother began to experience deep emotional problems ranging from abandonment issues, depression, and all that comes with being deserted by her mother and left with an abusive father at the age of ten years old. And as if that was not traumatic enough, her father would not allow her to attend the local school.

PASTOR CK: That is so sad. What happened to your grandmother?

DAVID: She ended up marrying again, according to Auntie Doris. She had another daughter, my mother's half-sister.

I remember my mother telling me when I was much older that her father was the meanest man in the world. I suspect a lot of dark things happened in the house where she grew up for her to say something like that.

Mom did not talk a lot about her childhood. Many people lived in my grandpa's house and various confusing relationships were formed there. For example, my grandmother's cousin began having an intimate relationship with my grandfather.

Grandpa refused to allow my mom to go to church. They lived on a farm where they grew their own food, milked goats, and picked cotton.

When my grandmother was leaving, my mom recalled her fights with my grandpa. She had stayed as long as she could, through the violence, through the drinking, through his cheating on her and treating her like dirt. When she left, God blessed her to live a long rich life.

Mom got to see her mother only once again, just before she died. My mom at this point was sixty-five years old, and her mom had left her when she was only ten years old and had not gone back to see her since. Maybe she could not without consequence.

PASTOR CK: Tell me more about your mom. She lost her mother, was forbidden to attend school and church, had to work the farm, and watched her dad having illicit affairs. She did indeed have a rough childhood. What happened next?

DAVID: When she left home, Mom married a man named Eldred while she was still very young. They traveled together to California, hoping for new opportunities that the South did not offer people of color. I heard that my mom was so in love with him that there was not a place on earth she would not have followed him to.

Eldred had relatives in California. He would travel back and forth between Mississippi and Los Angeles in preparation for his family's eventual move there. When the time was right, he sold everything he had, thereby securing seed money to invest in making a living once he had established their new permanent residence.

In the meantime, he sent my mother to Chicago, along with my brother, Larry, to wait with relatives who lived there until he had prepared a place for them. Kathryn, my oldest sister, went to live with Eldred's mom until he had made everything ready for the family in Los Angeles.

I do not know how long they were in Chicago or what relatives they lived with, but I am sure that it was no longer than a year.

1954

PASTOR CK: So, was it an easy transition for the family?

DAVID: Eldred finally secured a place in Los Angeles on 58th and Hooper near Ascott. Sadly, after getting situated in their new home, enrolling my brother and sister in school, and Eldred's finding a new job, things began to change. My siblings said their dad developed what they called, "wandering eyes in the bright lights and big city..." He eventually lost sight of the very purpose for which he had convinced my mother to pack up the kids and move.

Eldred worked at the Steel Mill Company and my mom enjoyed staying home taking care of the kids and going to church. Her place of worship was the same as the famous gospel group called the Chambers Brothers, and so Sundays were exciting times. There was always a crowd because people wanted to hear the group sing.

While Mom stayed faithful at home raising her kids, she began to feel that Eldred was becoming more and more distant towards her. Even though the relationship was strained, they were still having kids. Next came Jonathan in 1958.

Light Skinned vs Dark Skinned

Then in 1960, my sister Daisy was born, and things got bad. Eldred questioned my mom as to whether Daisy was his baby.

PASTOR CK: Why was there a question?

DAVID: There was a strong prejudice against dark skin in his family. Eldred was dark and my sister Kathryn was light-skinned, and his mother did not like him because he was so dark – she preferred his lighter-skinned siblings.

Eldred decided that he would leave his family altogether (as he had been leading a double life) and move in with his mistress.

He did commit to my mother to take care of her and his children financially for as long as he could.

PASTOR CK: How did that work out? How painful that had to have been for your mother.

> My mom was left to be both mother and father to us.

DAVID: That did not last long at all, as his other woman soon gave him an ultimatum. He would have to choose between her and his family. She said, "It's either me or them... choose!" He, sadly, chose her. Therefore, the brook dried up for my mother and my siblings financially, leaving them to fend for themselves in a strange city with no friends, job, or family.

Mom, The Sole Provider

PASTOR CK: What did your mom do and how did she care for her children?

DAVID: Mom had to find work. My sisters tell me she was devastated and deeply brokenhearted, humiliated by her marital status -- separated and now on her way to being divorced.

This was not what she had signed up for. Eldred had promised her the world. He had committed to loving, caring for, and protecting his children and now that was all changed.

My mom was left to be both mother and father to us. With little work experience and no education, she was forced to become a domestic worker, cleaning other people's houses. Her house cleaning job could only cover so many bills and it got to the point where rent was higher than what she was bringing in. And so, another unexpected blow came when she had to move out of her house.

PASTOR CK: What would she do now with four kids and no housing?

DAVID: She ended up contacting Eldred and they agreed that my sister, Kathryn, would live with her grandmother and that everybody else would continue to live with her. I understand that my mother tried to find a place that would be appropriate and affordable, but she finally gave up in humiliation and she and my brother Larry had to move into a shelter. Her dignity and respect were all gone.

This was a very low point for my mother. Everything familiar and comfortable was stripped away, including her self-esteem. I heard from my older brother how this period in her life ripped her apart and caused her to morph into someone she had never dreamed of becoming. It was also hard on my siblings.

PASTOR CK: David, how does all of this make you feel, what kind of emotions are coming up for you as you tell your mother and siblings' story?

DAVID: You know, I'm sad about it. I did not fully realize what my mother had gone through back then. She had come from what we call "the country" or a rural area in Mississippi to the bright lights and big city of Los Angeles...was left alone, all on her own, with no family or friends to lean on. She was alone with four kids to take care of.

To be honest, I feel angry about that. The cheating destroyed her and that is when she started drinking to numb the pain. I, as a young boy, did not understand the struggle Mom faced at the time, but now I can see and understand clearly the seemingly impossible choices that she had to make. It not only destroyed her, but my brother Larry shared how it hurt him deeply to see his father treat his mother that way.

PASTOR CK: Eldred didn't consider the effect that his decision would have on the whole family, and that was not fair.

DAVID: Yeah, they went from place to place not having anywhere stable to live, never knowing how long they would be allowed to stay in any one location before being kicked out or asked to leave. It was sad, and it still hurts to think about it. Eldred lived comfortably and well with his woman while his wife and kids were living from pillar to post. And he was OK with that. Man!

PASTOR CK: Even now, I can see that those feelings are being stirred up in you, bringing sadness and pain. Remember, you are processing some of these things for the first time.

DAVID: True. Well, Eldred continued to work at the steel mill until he was able to fulfill his dream of opening his own restaurant, and from there he opened a second one. They were called the Blue Flame (a soul food spot on Slauson and Broadway), and the Sassy Cat (a strip joint) that his sister managed for him.

At some point, my brother Jonathan went to live with his father. It was impressive for a son to see his dad having his own business, but it would not overshadow the damage his father did to our mother. That's my mother's history and her story.

PASTOR CK: Not an easy journey at all for your mom and her children. My heart aches for her and so many moms like her who were left to try and make a decent living for themselves and their children.

In our next chapter, why don't we pick up where we left off, at the many addresses you wanted to talk about where you stayed?

CHAPTER 4

Childhood

DAVID: The second place I remember living was on 50th Street (off Central and Hooper). Regrettably, I accidentally burned that house down.

My sister Daisy said that she was at school when it happened. I was inside playing with matches, and somehow, I set a brown coat on fire.

I do not remember who was home with me. All I remember is that it went *whoooosh!* I ran outside, and before I made it through the front door, the house was up in flames. Mom was out front with our neighbor.

When she saw what had happened, she walked over to me, slapped me hard and screamed, "What are you doing?!" She was angry! I remember most of all that slap and how angry she was. I felt bad for burning the house down. I remember the firetrucks coming and every word she said to me.

Yet she did not want me to shoulder the blame, so she blamed the Hispanic neighbors next door for the fire. Thank God, nothing came of that accusation.

The Third House

The third house I remember us moving to was on 49th Street. I liked that our service porch was connected to a church, and you could look through the peephole and watch the preacher preach!

I used to make fun of the service and make jokes about the preacher, who happened to be a woman. It is too bad that I was watching from the outside, not understanding what was going on inside. If only Mom had taken us to church during that season, maybe her life and ours would be different.

Morning Time Is the Best Time

I always looked forward to spending time alone with my mom when she was home. The early mornings were our times before Aunt Ruthie and the crew came over. I would wake up and run to the kitchen where she was. Mom was nice then. I saw a different mom before I went to school, but only in the mornings. The drinking started after I left. That is why to this very day I cannot stand the smell of alcohol.

After 2 pm, she just could not stay home. She had so many influences in her life that pulled her away from us, the men and then Aunt Ruthie and the drinking crew. They all loved going to this joint called The Hole in the Wall on Central.

My mother's drinking didn't just impact us, but it also impacted those in our neighborhood. I was at school one day and one of my friends said to me, "I saw your mother drunk at The Hole in the Wall." He described how my mom was acting and how drunk she was. I wanted to punch him in his mouth. He was laughing and then the other kids started laughing with him. I felt so angry and embarrassed and there was nothing I could do about it. It was all true.

On another occasion, I remembered being at someone's house and hearing one of the kids there referring to my mother as "that lady that be drunk all the time." That hurt too. She had a reputation.

CHAPTER 5

Taunting Toys

Christmas time was my favorite holiday. I was filled with excitement imagining the toys I hoped to get, because Mom would always give us presents. This Christmas, however, was different, and changed how I looked at Christmas from then on. I remember it so clearly.

I was about six years old, and I remember playing with my friends Mitch and Joe after school. Mitch said, "Hey, my cousin has some toys in this vacant house down the street." So Mitch led the way and we took off running to go see the toys.

And that's where I met him, Mitch's cousin who was about seventeen or eighteen years old. I do not remember his name or what he looked like. I just remember that he was tall. His image is blurred to me.

As soon as Mitch saw his cousin, he said show us where the toys are. His cousin led us to a foul-smelling, dingy, dark beige-brown room. I can still remember that smell today. I only remember the bed where the toys were. At first, we were all looking at the toys together—hot rod cars, trucks, play guns, baseball hats and balls, footballs— and then the cousin sent Mitch and Joe to his house on an errand, and they took off running.

I looked up from playing with the toys on the bed and there he was, just standing staring down at me.

Then he grabbed me and threw me on the bed. I did not know what to do. Then he grabbed the lamp next to the bed showing it to me in one hand saying in a very angry voice, "I will bust your head with this lamp; and kill you if you tell anyone..." With his hand on my neck, he said, "If you move; I will kill you...So, don't move, don't yell, don't do anything!" Tears ran out of my eyes, and I did not know if he was going to whoop me or what I did wrong. He pulled my pants down and raped me. It hurt

> All I wanted to do
> was run and
> not ever stop.

so bad. I could not scream, I was hurting and scared at the same time.

I felt dirty and I could not wash it away. When he let me go, I ran and ran with no destination in mind. I just wanted to get away.

I did not know what shock was back then, but I remember walking as if I was in a fog, not able to figure things out. I felt scared all the time. I felt jumpy. For a long time, I was convinced that it was my fault. I just wanted to hide.

Two days later, I went over to Joe's house, and I found out that Mitch's cousin had done the same thing to him.

My mother did not know. It was my secret and that is how I wanted to keep it. I still remember the pain.

That experience traumatized me for years after that. I remember that one day as my mother was leaving, I lost it. In my mind I was remembering my pants being pulled down and it overwhelmed me. I could not defend myself! I screamed, "DON'T GO MOMMA, PLEASE!"

She paid no attention to my meltdown. I was left alone to comfort myself as I had become used to doing.

PASTOR CK: You felt so powerless.

DAVID: And the truth was, I was powerless. I could not make my mother stay home, just like I could not make the man stop abusing me. Imagine a giant block of cement pressing down on you...It felt like I was not in my body but outside looking on. I was jacked up for a long time after that. I was putting my hands through walls, and nobody knew why. All I wanted to do was run and not ever stop.

PASTOR CK: Earlier, we discussed how uncomfortable it was for you to allow people to hug you or for you to hug them. You implied that since being molested you were not comfortable with this kind of touching. How did this play out in your life?

DAVID: Well, if it was a male that wanted to embrace me, I would stiffen up, and act standoffish. It was very uncomfortable and embracing another male was not easy for me to do.

I remember one day when my biological father came over, the first thing he tried to do was embrace me. I flinched and became distant. I did not notice this side of me until I was much older.

My family upbringing did not include affection, like holding hands and saying things like, "I love you" or "You mean so much to me." So, the intimacy of touching someone, whether physically or emotionally, was awkward for me. Then, after I was molested, I was afraid for anyone to hug me or hold me.

PASTOR CK: That's why you may remember me sharing, it might be a good idea to find a therapist to talk about these deeper matters. It's one thing to uncover them, and another thing to live with what you have uncovered. It's hard work what you are doing in writing your book, I strongly advise additional support during this time. It will only help your healing process.

God gave us counselors, pastors, psychologists, and therapists, all for the equipping and healing of his people. God knows we live in a broken society, and broken people break people.

DAVID: Yes, I believe we should get the help we need. I want to discuss more about my childhood.

PASTOR CK: You lead the way.

CHAPTER 6

Angels are Real

DAVID: At school, I was constantly embarrassed about one thing or another. The teacher, however, that I am thinking about right now is Ms. Lewis.

I believe Ms. Lewis was one of my angels, sent to strengthen me. She was a brown-skinned, afro-hair-style-wearing, older lady. She was the grandmother that I never had who would hug me daily. She would come to my house to check up on me and sometimes bring me brand new shoes (hush puppies) which I needed. I would be leaping with joy and excitement as if it were Christmas. If I had been good in the classroom, she would give me soybeans.

One day I was fighting in her class, and while trying to kick this kid I ended up kicking her. She started crying, and boy, I have never felt so bad in all my life!

Another day she came to our house and heard me calling my sister Black. When I saw her, I was so ashamed. She just smiled and said, "Now, David, you just complimented your sister. It's a wonderful thing to be a strong Black woman. I know you did not mean it as an insult. Now go ahead and apologize in case she thought you were trying to insult her. Go on, say sorry."

I did just what she said, and I felt so good. She was my authoritarian who loved me unconditionally. She would pinch my jaws and I loved all the attention she gave me. She validated me, and to her, I was not invisible. She would hug me and that would make me feel as though I mattered.

PASTOR CK: Ms. Lewis was an angel you say, sent from God. That suggests that what you are without at home, God will make a way to still fulfill - especially those basic needs of affirmation, love, validation and physical holding.

DAVID: That's right. I only wished she could have moved in, or I could have become her son.

Teacher from Hell

Then I had another teacher, Ms. Thomas. She had plastic surgery appointments to have her skin tightened. It was obvious to those of us who knew the before and after. She would say some horrible things to me. Of course, I was a kid who was always defending himself, a kid who frequented the principal's office for disciplinary purposes, a kid who was often caught fighting and acting out...a kid who was very unhappy at home.

One time I was talking in class, and Ms. Thomas put a dunce cap on me – identifying that the wearer either had ringworms or was unintelligent, and the kids all laughed at my expense. I felt like everybody was talking and laughing about what had happened to me, in class and out. It felt like they all called me names.

Ms. Thomas sent me on frequent trips to the principal's office for discipline.

This is how the punishment worked:

- If you were fighting... 16 swats

- If you were talking... 8 swats

- Usually, if I got into trouble, the principal would make me wait in his office during lunch. I was often full from eating when he came in after running errands. He would take out his paddle and chase me around the office as I screamed: "No, no, no...." I knew every detail of his office décor.

CHAPTER 7

Father Complications

DAVID: One night, my mom and Aunt Ruthie were in the kitchen talking, and I heard Aunt Ruthie say something very confusing. She sounded mad. "That boy looks like my brother from head to toe. That ain't Sean's boy and you know it. So, stop spreading that lie!" Mom just put down her head and did not say anything back. Sean happened to be an old man. I was told by my mom that Sean was my dad when I was about six years old. Aunt Ruthie was not having it.

I may have been too young to process it, but Aunt Ruthie's words never left me. That was not the only time she said it. Aunt Ruthie was the firecracker in the family and boy, did she live up to her nickname.

She was a very tall, stout-built woman, who always wore a big wig and loud clothes. Aunt Ruthie had to have her comfortable shoes, though. She walked on the backs of them sometimes, and you could see her hard, ashy, cracked heels.

There were times as a little boy when Aunt Ruthie would pull me to the side and whisper, "My brother is your daddy, don't forget that." I did not know what she wanted me to do. Maybe she just wanted me to know something.

All I knew was I saw two different men that lived at the house from time to time. I remember Jimmy living in the house with my mom when Sean was not there. It seemed Sean and Jimmy took turns room-mating.

From time to time, I learned that my real dad (Jimmy) would come over and leave, but my mom kept Sean always as a spare. From what I could understand, Sean was a provider for my mom and he helped her with her bills like rent, utilities, and whatever she needed. She cared for him, but she also wanted to be with Jimmy, my dad, who was not the settling down type, being a "rolling stone" (as they called them back in the day).

PASTOR CK: There is a pattern here: Your mom was attracted to men who were not available either emotionally or physically.

DAVID: Yeah, the men she was attracted to, she had to chase. Those that were chasing her, she was not really feeling all that much, but they were serving a purpose in her life.

So, Sean was the provider for the family and would give her the world, while Jimmy only wanted the physical part of my mom. To be honest, I thought Sean was my dad because I was always around his family.

One day, Aunt Ruthie came over while Sean was in the kitchen, and she just blurted out real loud to my mom, "Look at that boy, he looks just like my brother Jimmy Anderson. Hmm, you can't deny it!" Sean looked at my mom sadly. I never understood why Aunt Ruthie would front him like that. I would usually be in the background looking at the TV or something during these outbursts and arguments.

Sean did not have a car, so he walked everywhere. When she said that, he just walked right out of the house.

The Meeting

Then the day came when Aunt Ruthie and Jimmy were at the house on the same afternoon. Aunt Ruthie started shouting, "That boy looks just like you Jimmy..." He stood there in the living room, looking down at me with a funny smile on his face. It was almost like he was caught.

After that day, I would see Jimmy more at the neighborhood store, Zabbys. Jimmy liked to drink with his buddies on the corner. I believed in my heart that he saw the resemblance and in subtle ways tried to be my dad. He started giving me money to buy treats at the store and acknowledging me.

Then I learned I had sisters and brothers around the corner. These were Jimmy's children.

For my mom, it was all confusing and probably embarrassing in some way, because she was seeing both men and being intimate at the same time, which made it hard for her to know who my father was. It was complicated.

When I would see Sean in public on the streets, it would be like he did not see me. He would not speak or talk with me. There was no connection that a father and son would have.

One day I was at Aunt Ruthie's, and Jimmy was there. He asked me to go to the store with him and for the first time, I felt a connection. He ran into a friend while we were at the store and introduced me as his son.

I could not even explain what went through me when he said that. I felt affirmed, validated, and like somebody wanted me. I had my father finally, at the age of eight years old.

This was so important to me because I used to watch my other siblings interact with their dad Eldred and it would make me so sad not to have the same kind of relationship.

Eldred, My Siblings' Father

Eldred used to come to the house and pick up his kids and leave me there. I would cry because they had a dad, and I didn't have one.

At times, Eldred would come to give his children gifts but not me. It was so painful.

There were days that Eldred would take Larry and Jonathan a lot, but not Daisy. He had favorites even among his own kids.

When Daisy and Jonathan would leave to be with their father, it would trigger something very deep within me. It felt like they were wanted by their dad, and I was not. They were chosen, but I was not. Do you know what it feels like to not be picked or chosen? It feels like, "He is not good enough, we don't want him around." Eldred would express his love and give them money right in front of me, and I would get nothing. It was a lonely feeling and an empty place.

I remember my mom giving me a quarter to try and make things better for me. I would go down the street to the store to get some candy after they left with their father.

My dad Jimmy and my mom had something in common: they could not stay in one place long. I hated that about my mom, and now I found myself hating that about my dad. I wanted to see him all the time and every day.

CHAPTER 8

A Man Named Barry

DAVID: The next mystery man that showed up at our house weeks later was a man named Barry. Mom just came out and said he was her boyfriend and would be around.

Barry turned out to be a good father figure. He seemed to be more stable and cared for my mom.

He treated us with respect and generosity. His presence was consistent, and he even convinced Mom to stay home more than she typically would. Life changed in our household, and it felt like a stable family at first.

We enjoyed going to the drive-ins on Friday nights in his red station wagon. He had nieces and nephews who would come along too. We were sort of like a big family around him, which was much different from all the other men. They just wanted Mom's time and had nothing to do with us.

I saw something very different in both him and my mom. They were openly affectionate toward one another. He would hug my mom and tell her he loved her in front of us. That made me feel good to see her happy.

When the 1971 earthquake came, Barry was there and he kept us calm, telling us, "We are going to be okay." He was right, we were okay. He stood by and made sure we were all together. He made sure we were safe.

I remember getting into his shoes – he was tall, broad, and big...not a loud guy. He would shout, "Get out of my shoes, boy!" I would laugh and run.

We lived for the weekend with Barry because he took us to the Vermont Drive-in and on Saturdays to the Pike.

Stuck in the Trunk

Barry also had an old Buick that he kept parked in front of the house. One day, his nephew was hanging out with me when I came up with the bright idea of getting into the trunk of the car. We did and the stupid

> He did not know it, but he showed me how much he cared.

boy pulled it closed on us. Needless to say, we immediately realized that this was a bad idea. Locked in the trunk, we started screaming like girls. Thank God, this man was walking by, and heard the noise and ran to the house to get my mother. She ran out, popped the trunk, and proceeded to whoop our butts!

Barry lit into us and told us we had better never do that again. "You could have suffocated in that trunk if nobody was walking by," he said. He did not know it, but he showed me how much he cared.

I was happy for a season, more than I had been in a long time, because of the consistency in Mom and her new boyfriend Barry.

Change Couldn't Last

I guess the lifestyle of being at home kind of got to her over time. Mom started slipping back out to hang out with Mary and Aunt Ruthie. I could not believe it. "Why go back to that way of living?" I thought. "We have a perfect family now." I started getting mad at her. Barry was not the partying type, and he did not want Mom to go out and drink either. He told her that. Mom would listen, but as soon as he had to work or go somewhere; she hit the streets. He would come back and find her gone. Boy, he would boil. We saw it. He did not say too much other than "Where's your momma?"

Barry was very jealous – he didn't like Aunt Ruthie and Mary, or the girls coming to get Mom to party on the weekend. Barry would come home and she would be gone, and eventually, he left.

Mom would come home, and they would argue about going and leaving and coming home drunk and late. He hung around for about a year. Kathryn, my sister, told me she would mess with a lot of men.

Fighting in the Car

One day my mom and I were in Barry's car; I do not know what they were talking about, but the next thing I knew Barry was grabbing my mother. Barry threw a blow and hit her. My mom was fighting back hard. I reached over the seat and bit him on his arm, and he stopped. My mother's mouth was busted, and she was crying. Seeing the blood coming from my mother's mouth made me feel helpless. I was crying and telling him, "Please don't hit my momma anymore."

I did not know what to do. I began to holler at him, "I hate you, I hate you."

"I hate you too," he said back. We got out of the car. Barry drove off fast. All night I remember wondering to myself, how can a man hit a woman like she was a man? How could he have hurt my mom like that? What did she do to deserve that? I couldn't understand. I had complicated feelings about Barry: even though he hit my mom, with him I had finally felt like I belonged, and someone wanted me to be part of their life.

Weeks went by and Mom's face was bruised for a while. It hurt me each time I saw her. I could see that day like it just happened. She suffered another broken heart. I hated seeing my mother so sad, but I also really missed Barry. He was the best father figure I had. When he left, I felt so lost and empty. It impacted everyone in the house.

For all his faults, Barry helped me trust in a man. I never felt afraid around him, I never felt hesitant or questioned his affection for me. I believed he loved me like a father loves a son. So, how could he leave us just like that?

CHAPTER 9

Girls

DAVID: My first intimate encounter with a girl was when I was nine years old. My next-door neighbor approached me–she was older than me, probably about fourteen or fifteen.

I was friends with her brother Roy, and they would pick us up and take us to church on the neighborhood bus. Roy had three sisters. I did not know it at the time, but Roy's sister was looking at me and sizing me up for her plans. Then one day it happened. Roy and his family had left the house and only Lisa and I were left.

While we were on the back porch, she started saying things I did not understand at the time. "David, why don't you come inside the house with me? I want to show you something in my room." Those were scary words, and I was not sure how to respond, but I followed her.

The next thing I knew she was kissing me, pulling my pants down, and then we were on her bed. I did not know what to do, but she guided my hands to touch her body, and everything started. It felt good. It felt different, and I liked how she handled me and wanted to be with me like that.

That day led to many more days of the same thing. She took my virginity, and I became sexually active at a young age. I became so attached to her. She was pretty. I loved her long hair and her light skin tone. Her eyes were brown and sexy. Her body was cute, she was built like a woman. She would tell me how cute I was to her. I was her favorite Hershey Bar. It was like I thought about her all the time and what we were doing was always on my mind.

We would see each other every day and would start having sex as soon as I got home from school. She waited for me. "What took you so long?" she would say sometimes.

That made me feel like a man in a way I had never felt before. She wanted me and I liked the closeness.

One day, my worst fears were realized. We were caught! We hid in a closet on the service porch and all of a sudden, her stepfather opened the closet door looking for clothes or something.

We were praying that he wouldn't look down, but he did, and he saw us. He yelled, "Boy if you don't get yo ass out of here! What are you guys doing?" Lisa said, "Nothing!" He couldn't wait for my mother to come home to tell her. I got a whooping that night from my mother. Boy did she wear me out.

The next thing I knew, Lisa was not coming straight home anymore. I wondered what was going on with her. I learned she had a boyfriend her age when I saw her get out of his car. I was devastated because I thought I was the one she loved. The sex we were having every day made me feel like I was the special one in her life.

Her boyfriend would come over there and I would see her talking to him on the porch where she used to talk to me. I was upset. It was the first time I had ever felt jealousy over a girl, and I did not have anybody to talk to about those feelings of anger and a broken heart. Yet we continued being intimate. I pretended I was not fazed at all by him. I could not say no, because I guess my ego was involved, and deep down I thought I could take her away from him. She would call me over and I would always go. I was willing to play second fiddle.

Even so, something was not feeling right. I did not like it, but I did not know how to express myself because I was so young. Plus, I just wanted to be with her, and so I was willing to keep going over there to be with her despite her boyfriend.

PASTOR CK: This relationship started when you were nine. How long did it last and how did it affect your relationship with girls after that?

DAVID: It only lasted that year, but it ignited something in my body. I was sexually active from that time on. I must confess that I did not know how to treat a girl. I was nice to them if they pleased me, but I never had an example showing me how to act in a relationship and so I did what I had seen acted out before me. Mom left home a lot and that allowed me to bring girls over. We never had to worry about parental interruption, because she didn't come back until everyone was asleep.

PASTOR CK: David, what comes up for you from talking about this subject?

DAVID: I wish I had a different foundation and a different example of how to treat girls, women, and relationships. For me, they were just sexual objects. They were for my gratification alone. I had such a selfish perspective and girls got hurt because of my bent perspective. I regret that.

When I look in hindsight, I see that I would have done things differently if I had the guidance and tools.

CHAPTER 10

Running

PASTOR CK: Let's talk about your past times as a young boy. What hobbies did you have or enjoy? Were you involved in sports?

DAVID: It is crazy to be bored out of your mind. You know, Mom was not around much after school. So, Will (Aunt Ruthie's son) and I would hang out and do the craziest things.

Aunt Ruthie had three boys. One night, Will and I went up to the Conner Johnson Mortuary where a neighbor worked. He would let us in to view the dead bodies. The mortuary was just off Avalon. I don't know why that was fun for us. I guess we loved it because it grossed our friends out when we told them about it. It was like a scary movie.

Will was 12 or 13 years old, and I had to be about 11. You may not believe this, but we would touch the bodies and pretend they were threatening and chasing us.

Let me tell you another story about my cousins Will and Marty. I was not there, but another cousin told me about Will and Marty's last fight. They were wrestling with each other as they tussled over a gun. The gun went off and Will ended up killing Marty. Will was devastated. He couldn't believe that Marty was dead. He cried and cried but it was too late. He could not take it back.

Even now, it is hard to remember that day. I loved those guys. They were both my best friends and cousins. My other cousin, who was there, said, "The hurt in Will's eyes after it happened was hard to look at. He held Marty and rocked him like a baby saying over and over, 'I'm sorry, I'm sorry, I'm sorry!'"

PASTOR CK: How did this affect you?

DAVID: It hurt me. I could not believe it. I knew them both and Will was only fourteen years old when he was sent to prison for it. I lost them both at one time. I felt so empty.

After this, I stopped going over to Aunt Ruthie's house and stayed closer to the neighborhood with my friend Nathan from school. What I loved about Nathan as a friend was that he lived with both of his parents, and they had such a cool family. His mother treated me like I was her son. His parents invited me to go with them wherever they were going if I happened to be at the house. No matter where we went, they would introduce me as their son. She made me feel loved like I wanted my mom to make me feel. It was almost like God put her in my life to fulfill those areas my mom could not. At times, I secretly wished that she was my mother.

My favorite road trip was when we visited her brother in La Puente, CA. He had this big swimming pool, and we had so much fun eating and swimming. Her brother had two daughters, and I always looked forward to going over there and playing with them. The hardest part of those weekends was coming back home. I never really knew what I would come home to.

This one time, I came back home from having a fun-filled weekend with Nathan's family and found a strange man in the house with my mother, Mary, and Ruthie.

Something was wrong and I could feel it when I walked in. I quickly learned that this guy had been arguing with my mother. Before I knew it, I jumped right into it, telling him, "You can't make my mother do anything or go anywhere she doesn't want to."

I got up in the man's face at the age of eleven years old and when it was all said and done, my mother grabbed her purse and said, "Let's get out of here!" In our estimation, she chose him over her kids, and we did not see her again for a couple of days. I could not understand what my mother was doing.

PASTOR CK: You took it personally and you were disappointed that once more, she chose someone else, a stranger even, over you and your siblings? What were you feeling?

DAVID: Mainly frustration and things I could not even put into words. I began to see a pattern in my mother. I did not want to believe certain things about my mother because they did not make me feel good. I do not even know where she met him and where he came from. After that day, I never saw him again.

PASTOR CK: Running became part of a theme for you as well, did it not? You would run physically, emotionally, and mentally when frustrated and afraid?

DAVID: I guess so. It's like when I would be in a classroom – in those special classes. If I were embarrassed about something, I would walk out of class.

> I am no longer afraid,
> I am no longer ashamed,
> and I am no longer powerless.
> I have Jesus Christ who is my vindicator!
> He has vindicated me!

When I look back at it, even though I did not realize it then, I was suffering from anxiety disorder. My hands used to shake violently, especially if I were in a situation where someone was standing over me and focusing totally on me. I did not like being touched or the center of someone's attention. I felt that my back was up against a wall. I did not like anyone to hug me, only my mom.

PASTOR CK: Did you ever tell your siblings or your parents?

DAVID: No never. I was too ashamed, too afraid.

PASTOR CK: Why now?

DAVID: It is time now. I am no longer afraid, I am no longer ashamed, and I am no longer powerless. I have Jesus Christ who is my vindicator! He has vindicated me! I want to give witness to other boys and men who have been where I have been and need validation and healing. I want to point them to the cross where all my shames were nailed!

CHAPTER 11

School Years

PASTOR CK: Let's continue looking at your school years. Tell me more about them.

DAVID: At first, school was good for me because there were other kids and I liked being with people. One teacher comes to mind. She was so nice to me in the beginning. Over time, however, she changed on me. She would call on me and sometimes I did not have the answers because I did not have my homework finished.

My mother was not available to go over lessons with me and I did not have anyone else to help. As a result, I could hardly read and was barely able to write.

One day this teacher crushed me. She needed me to answer her questions accurately. I struggled. I tried and I failed to meet her standards. "You're dumb! You're stupid! If you haven't learned how to read and write by now, you are never going to learn." These words flew out of her mouth without hesitation as if she had been holding back all this time, expressing what she truly felt about me and how she saw me.

I had nowhere to hide, nowhere to run, and the kids all started laughing at me. The whole school year, I had to hear those words from the kids and my teacher. It felt like things were getting worse and worse, so I did not want to go to school anymore. I woke up daily filled with the dread of what she might say about me, and then what the kids might say about me afterwards. I started acting out. I was fighting, I was angry, and I would get into trouble and end up in the principal's office a lot.

PASTOR CK: You didn't have anywhere to hide from the shame and humiliation, and it turned into anger and rage.

DAVID: I did not know why she was picking on me. It felt so unnecessary, I just wanted to die. Then the kids started calling me Dirty David because my clothes were dirty, and my shoes had holes in them. I believed that I was dumb and stupid; I could not write, I could not read like everyone else. My name changed – I was now Dirty David. Many times, I just wished I could disappear.

PASTOR CK: Your teacher was a bully. The kids followed her example. You didn't have a chance with them. I'm so sorry you experienced that level of damaging treatment.

DAVID: Damaging is a perfect word, I felt like a damaged boy with lots of defects.

PASTOR CK: How did this impact the rest of your adolescent years?

DAVID: So much of that period is blank and I cannot remember a lot about it. I think that, because life was so painful, maybe I have buried the pain down deep, and I do not even think I want it to come up. But I was determined that one day I would read and write the way I should.

I taught myself through reading the Bible. I was not illiterate, but I was way behind my class in my formative years. The Lord helped me.

I read the Psalms. I do not know where the desire came from, but I remember that I was drawn to the Psalms. My prayer went something like this, "Lord, You have to help me to learn to read, please! You have to show me how!" And he did.

PASTOR CK: This is so powerful. You triumphed over all you had to go through with the help of the Lord!

DAVID: Yes! And He is still my Helper today.

CHAPTER 12

Good Memories

PASTOR CK: David, tell me about some of your good memories. We talked about God leaving a "handful" of purposes strategically to strengthen you for the journey. Tell me more about some of these things.

DAVID: Well, there was this deacon at Mt. Zion Baptist Church on 52nd and Hooper that would pick me up and take me to church. He cared about me. The pastor of that church baptized me one Sunday. The deacon and his wife both have since passed away. He would pick me up and take me to different churches to sing in a trio composed of myself, another little boy, and a girl. We all lived on 49th Street. I lived in that location from the age of 6 to 19.

Deacon had us memorize scriptures, and the one that comes to mind right now is Psalm 103. He taught us to praise the Lord all the time and not just in church. He told us that there are benefits to doing this and they are forgiveness for all our sins and healing of all our diseases.

Psalm 103 NIV
Of David.

> *¹ Praise the Lord, my soul;*
>   *all my inmost being, praise his holy name.*
> *² Praise the Lord, my soul,*
>   *and forget not all his benefits—*
> *³ who forgives all your sins*
>   *and heals all your diseases,*
> *⁴ who redeems your life from the pit*
>   *and crowns you with love and compassion,*
> *⁵ who satisfies your desires with good things*
>   *so that your youth is renewed like the eagle's.*

There was a cleaners in the back of my house. The owner and his wife took me to church also. He would allow me to work at the cleaners doing little odd jobs around there. He taught me responsibility and it felt great to have a job and someone depending on me.

We had this store across the street called Del Market and I also had favor with the owner there. She would allow me to do small jobs for her. I would deliver groceries to customers, and she paid me $3, gave me cookies and cuts of that thick salami rolled in paper.

I also remember my barber. Mom would tell me to get a covadis, a very close haircut, but the barber would say, "I am going to keep some hair on your head." My job was to clean the shop. It just so happens that this was the shop where our pastor got his hair cut. I would carry his briefcase when he came to town.

PASTOR CK: It is good to know that some adults in your life served as an example of the love of God. God placed the right people in just the right places at just the right time in your life.

DAVID: Yes!

> I want to thank you, Lord, that You love me enough that You sent people into my life all along the way to let me know that I am not worthless. People that convinced me not to give up. You sent men into my life to introduce me to Your love and word at an early age - Men that saw my worth... Men that encouraged my gifting... You do all things well! Thank You, Father, in the mighty and matchless name of Jesus!
> Amen.

CHAPTER 13

My Brother Larry

PASTOR CK: God has been good to you, David. He brought you through a lot of tough situations safely and healed the resulting scars. Tell me about your brothers and sisters. Did they experience similarly difficult times?

DAVID: Larry, my oldest brother, lived between my mom and his dad. He used to whip my butt from time to time. One day I went under the house for some reason and cracked the pipes and he let me have it. Then he told mom, and she whipped me again.

Larry would have parties at the house frequently and charge his friends from Jefferson High an entry fee of twenty-five cents to get in. He would tell us to stay in our room, but of course, we would sneak out to see what was going on. Girls would come to the back door asking us to help them sneak in, and we did. This went on every other Friday. Ours was a pretty big house and so there were lots of kids there. Al Green (Let's Stay Together), Marvin Gaye (I Heard It Through the Grapevine), and the Staple Sings (I'll Take You There) could be heard blasting all over the neighborhood. Thank God nobody called the police. Larry was very popular and so he had lots of girlfriends. He was a sharp dresser and wore a big afro.

Kathryn, my oldest sister, spent most of her time with her grandmother, aunt, and dad. She did not live with us for the most part. Jonathan lived with his father primarily. Larry was back and forth, going between our house and his father's. Danny, Daisy, and I lived with Mom our whole juvenile lives.

CHAPTER 14

Lasting Effects of Child Abuse

PASTOR CK: David, you were abused physically, emotionally and sexually in your childhood. How do you think it affected your outlook on the world, your perception of self and your relationships?

DAVID: I must say that I was warped personally. I was constantly fearful that I was not good enough, that people would make fun of me, or that I could not depend on or trust that people would remain in my life. I was probably not the most patient person either. I was truly a product of my environment.

Children are sponges. They are a composite of all the deposits made by parents, siblings, teachers, and all the people who spoke into their lives in their developing years, negatively or positively. Let me just give you a list of some of the things I pondered as I went through counseling. People will tell you to "do as I say do and not as I do," but that is not how it works. Kids are watching authority figures, and the authority figures are the models or patterns that show them how to live their lives.

This is How Visuals Work for Kids

- What they are observing is shaping the way they think.

- It is shaping the way they react.

- It is shaping the way they respond to pressure.

- It is shaping their belief system.

- It shapes their insecurities.

- It shapes their coping mechanisms.

- It shapes their view of God.

- It shapes the kid's identity – the kid is looking to that father for problem-solving.

- He wants attention.

- He wants love.

- He wants approval.

- He wants security.

- He wants stability.

I have figured out one reason God hates divorce. Children do not have that father's covering that He designed them to need. In marriage, two become one flesh. Dad has his strengths and Mom has hers. Together, they have all that is needed to make the unit complete, to make it as God intended, for the children to grow up healthy mentally, physically, and emotionally. When this unit is disrupted, spiritual doors are opened that should have remained locked.

When there is a missing parent, kids wonder:

- Where are my mommy and daddy?

- Why don't I have a mom to talk to?

- Why can't I see my father every day?

- Why doesn't my father come to my school?

- Why doesn't my father play with me?

- Why doesn't my father love taking me fishing?

- Why didn't my daddy protect me?

It saddens me that my daddy was not there. I tried not to think about it because it made me very unhappy. I often daydreamed about what it would have been like to have a dad around– a dad that cared about me, a dad that loved me. I imagined us hanging out together and him taking me places. He would protect me, and, in my dreams, I was not scared anymore. Then, I would brush it off and get back to my real world. As a kid, I lived in a world of imagination and music. That, I believe, is the vehicle God used to keep me sane.

PASTOR CK: David, you have really thought this through. I admire that.

DAVID: Yeah, I experienced all the above-mentioned problems at one time or another. I would put on a mask because I wanted no one else to know. God told me to take off the mask and be willing to be naked and exposed, to show who I used to be and who I am now, that "hitherto, the Lord has brought me." He advised me that the world would not approve but He is the only one that counts.

CHAPTER 15

GIRLS AT THE HOUSE

DAVID: By the time I was fourteen years old, I had girls coming to my house. It was OK now for me to bring them home. Mom was OK with it. We jokingly called them my babysitters. I brought girl after girl to the house. I needed the attention. But looking back, even with all that attention, I still felt empty and alone.

PASTOR CK: Do you want to talk about any particular girl?

DAVID: Jessie was a year older than me, and she was the love of my life. I met her in high school. If memory serves correctly, she was in the 11th grade, and I was in 10th grade.

We were together until she graduated and then she left to go to college, breaking my heart into a thousand little pieces. Losing her was big. It reminded me of again, my mother leaving me and abandoning me. I know deep in her heart she did not know what I was struggling with, but I could not shake the feeling that was all too familiar to me.

She was the longest relationship I had, and it seemed like this was the most serious relationship. We would go out and spend lots of time together. I felt intimidated because she was college-bound and I was afraid she would find someone on her level. This made me even more insecure.

After she left, I adopted a new attitude that said, "I am going to hurt you before you hurt me." No one else was going to leave me anymore. I took on a callous attitude and I became promiscuous to get rid of the feeling of being so empty.

Every now and then when she would come back home, I would see her in different places. I had changed a lot since she was away at college. I started looking at other girls through a lens of what I could get only to benefit my needs. Admittedly I was needy for attention and validation, but I did not want to put my whole heart out there anymore for anyone.

I also was exposed to drugs around this time. It started with my brother Danny. He was selling with Joe. I became fascinated with the whole lifestyle, with cars, money, clothes, and women.

One day I got up the nerve to ask my brother to let me in on the opportunity. He did not want me to get involved, but he saw how determined I was, so he shielded me as much as possible. My brother was a large mover and shaker and he had to keep his distance from me because some would possibly compromise our safety.

My entrance into selling came when he entrusted me with one ounce of crack cocaine and told me to take it and give him half of what I sold. I learned how to cook it because he always came to my mom's house to cook his dope. He would bring his bottle and scale and I would watch him and that was my on-the-job training. I would know how to rock up a whole ounce and put it on the scale.

I flipped the money and made more than he expected. I was good with him because I gave him his money on the top. I learned how to make my rocks smaller and make more money. I was caught up over the money—an ounce was $800, and I would make $1600, and boy did it start getting good to me.

Before I knew it, I had so many clients and I eventually started with a half-kilogram. I worked with them at the spot making about $2,000 every other day. Once the operation started getting big, I would buy directly from my brother, and he would front me a half and I would sell ounces.

My clientele came straight from the neighborhood. It gave me a sense of importance, acceptance, respect, responsibility, and visibility.

PASTOR CK: You gained a lot.

DAVID: It brought a monster out of me that says "I'm the s@*)!it! I'm not invisible anymore and I am important!" I was a risk-taker, and I was not thinking of anybody else but myself and all the money I could make.

One day comes to mind, when this lady had her kids and came up to me to buy drugs. She sent her ten-year-old son to get drugs, and I saw it all. It jacked me up and it did something to me inside.

From 1984 to 1988 I sold crack cocaine. My car inventory was awesome. My brother gave me a 1964 White Cadillac with a turquoise top and bows. My next was a gray BMW which I bought cash, then a gray El Camino.

The next component of this lifestyle was the women I attracted. My first girl was Tiffany, who was from the neighborhood. I was in my 1976 Camaro with my rims and sounds blasting. I rolled up on her and asked her if she needed a ride. She said yes and hopped in the car.

From that day forward, we started spending time together. She had a young son, and the dad would come over, and I would wonder if they were still together.

She would come over to my mom's house. I was about nineteen years old. Tiffany would spend the night. She was a smoker of cigarettes; her mother would come through and get drugs from me as well. When I went over to Tiffany's house she would say, "Bring a gram with you, I got some customers for you."

The lifestyle brought many dangerous turns and unexpected events in my life. It came with the territory, we used to say.

Life with Tiffany had its share of drama. Looking back on our journey together, I was able to put different pieces together that she was betraying me – for example, she pretended to be away for the weekend but she was with her son's father. She pretended that nothing was going on between the two of them. But every time I was around, he had an attitude. I would say to myself, "If ain't nothing going on, why are you mad?"

One day he grabbed her in front of me and we began to fight. I was protecting her and did not mind being her security. Another day we were driving to the store, and I saw him again. I jumped out of my car to beat him up when I saw another guy coming near me with a gun. At the last minute, he recognized who I was. "Ah man, that's Dave," he said, turning away from me.

The lifestyle brought many dangerous turns and unexpected events in my life. It came with the territory, we used to say.

I started noticing my girl was losing lots of weight, scary weight, and quickly. Tiffany told me her mom introduced her to primos (rock cocaine mixed with weed). She said, "I just do it every now and then; I haven't done it in a long time."

One day I checked my stash, and it kept getting smaller and smaller. Tiffany had been tapping my stash. I wanted to catch her in the act so I pretended that I needed to make a run and so I jumped in my car and parked it around the corner and peeked through my window. She went straight to the stash and was taking my rocks. I busted her right then and there! I grabbed her and before I knew it, I slapped her. She had betrayed me, and I could not trust her. It did something to me.

I told her to get out of my house! She cried and begged, but I was angry. She eventually left but the aftermath was crazy.

She and her girls started doing jacked-up stuff, like driving by and throwing bricks in my window or stopping by my car and putting sugar in my tank. She was crazy!

CHAPTER 16

My First Serious Girlfriend

DAVID: One day a friend and I went up to Fox Hills Mall to hang out; he liked his custom-made Volkswagen with rims and sounds. That day, we left Fox Hill Mall early and drove down Crenshaw Blvd. to see when the girls got out of school. We were bumping sounds and getting the ladies' attention.

As we turned down 54th Street making a right, we pulled up near 8th Avenue and there she was, walking. My friend pulled over to talk with this lady. We learned her name was Sharon.

My friend was excited, and he gave his best shot at getting her attention. At first, I was sitting in the car, and then I jumped out to talk with her too. She looked at me and we began to talk, and she gave me more attention than she was giving him.

She had long, black hair down to her shoulder. When I jumped out, my friend fell back, giving me the lead. I got her number that day, and that night I called her and ended up at her house a few hours later.

From that night onward, we were a number, but in the meantime, Tiffany still rode by to see if anyone was at my house.

One night we were riding in my car, and Tiffany's sister saw us. She called Tiffany to let her know. Tiffany came around to the house and threw a brick at my car and ran off. We heard the noise and got up to see what was happening. Shocked, I explained to Sharon that this was a girl who liked me, but I was not interested. Luckily, she went for it.

I must admit, I enjoyed being with Sharon, taking her to the movies, and hanging out. I met her mom eventually, and she was using substances just like Tiffany's mom. She would try to get a deal or manipulate me since she knew I was a dealer.

Now, Sharon also had a sister who was heavily on drugs. Sharon did not mess with drugs or drink, or smoke. She was a straight girl and different from her sister and mother. She did not like the fact that her mother messed with drugs, so she enjoyed spending the night at my house. Her mother had a standard that said, "If you go spend the night out, it is time for you to get out."

Sharon and my mom were cool with each other. I was happy my mom liked her. Yet I found myself getting overprotective of Sharon and jealous. I remember one time one of my regular customers started flirting with her. I got angry and I told her, "Look I don't play that *@&it." I was not about to be dumped, played on, or betrayed again, like Tiffany did to me.

Another time, a guy I was selling to was trying to get at her, and she would smile back. Yet I still went to the club and did one-night stands here and there. Sharon would know what I was doing. Eventually, she knew the different numbers that popped up in my pager were not just drug deals but also other women. I was unfaithful and I was not right when it came to how I treated her and the relationship we had. This had major implications further down the road.

One night after I took her home, she and her mom got into a fight; she called me right back and said her mom told her to "get out." I went to get her, and she moved in and finished her senior year. Before we knew it, she was pregnant at seventeen, as soon as she started the 12th grade.

If she caught me cheating, I would flip it on her and go off as if she was in the wrong. I would feel like, "How dare you judge me." Sometimes, I would hit her. She would cry and I knew I was wrong.

When I think about it now, I can see that it would happen the most when I was triggered. Eventually, she took off and went to stay with her friend because she did not want to go back to her mother's house. Every time we fought, I told her to leave and go be with her friend. Yet I always called her, and she would end up coming back to the house...back and forth, back and forth.

Once my drugs flowed in more consistently, we got an apartment together. I was selling and customers would come over and knock on the door while Sharon and the baby were asleep.

One day, when our baby girl was about five months old, I was out and on my way back to the house. Sharon called me, saying the apartment was swarming with police officers. They wouldn't even let her in to get our baby's essentials while they searched our home. Amazingly, the police did not go to the bathroom – they would have seen a plate full of rocks on the toilet. Amazingly, the police did not go to the bathroom – they would have seen a plate full of rocks on the toilet.

I knew I had to get my family out of there, so we got another apartment on Budlong and Vernon, but I kept the other place to use when I needed it. I had two places where I was going back and forth. Women would come and buy, and I had a buddy who would help me run that spot over there.

In the meantime, while Sharon was at the other place, I would run with other women; and I would come home and give her diseases. She went through so much with me.

More Kids in the House

Sharon's sister Kim was getting deeper and deeper into drugs. She would bring her children over to the house, and we would keep them for her until she came back home.

We got a call one night to come to pick up her children. She had a traumatic experience and almost lost her life. We had to become their guardian and eventually, we adopted them. This also brought another level of strain to the household, but we loved them like our own. They went to school with the rest of the kids, and we were one big family.

Having a lot of children changes you. It makes you more alert, nervous, and sensitive. I remember one day I was in the house, and I heard this helicopter that sounded as if it kept getting closer and closer and closer. All I could think about was the children around the corner at the daycare and school. I ran out of the house and the helicopter crashed before my eyes. When the news covered the story, they said that if the pilot had not veered to the right, he could have crashed into the daycare. My heart was in my throat thinking about those kids. That was traumatizing, but God kept my kids.

A Lifestyle Getting Out of Control

I had a 78' Camaro with shining customized rims, turquoise and the works. One day I was over at my girlfriend Tiffany's house. I was crazy about my cars - I worshiped them. Suddenly, while I was cozying up to Tiffany, I heard this loud bang!

> My sister Daisy
> always would tell me
> that God had
> a plan for me.

Now all I had on were my silk pajamas (that all the high rollers wore) and slippers. I ran out of the house, and I saw this guy and his family in their car. They were the ones who hit my car. He saw me and took off. I jumped in my car and began chasing them down. He was hitting those corners so tight!

We were in an industrial area in Long Beach when I caught up with him. It was very dark. He stopped and I jumped out of my car and walked up to his: I noticed he had what looked like his whole family in the car and I was feeling cocky. The closer I approached the driver's side, the more I could see inside. Suddenly, I saw this shining chrome revolver, like a 357, slowly coming up; I froze and screamed, "Oh Lord, Oh Lord, please don't shoot me. Please don't shoot me."

I saw my life flash in front of my eyes. I ran so fast back to my car that I ran out of my slippers and sped off. My heart felt like it was beating in my throat at 100 miles an hour. That was my first close call to death.

I must admit that there were those in my life who kept telling me I had better get out of this life before I got killed or ended up in prison. My sister Daisy always would tell me that God had a plan for me. But I was addicted to the lifestyle and the fast money.

In fact, one day I decided I was going to go "cold turkey" and give up the life. I applied for a job at Big 5. I'll never forget when I got my first check: $400.00 for two weeks. My ego dropped to the ground.

I wanted to cry. That whole weekend I kept saying, "I can't do this. This is not enough money!" At the end of the month, I called my brother and told him I needed an ounce. I flipped it so fast I had several thousand dollars in my pocket.

I was back in the life again. Going "clean" didn't even last a whole month, but at least I tried. I patted myself on the back and acknowledged that working a regular job just was not for me at that time - I was too used to the fast money. I felt I was in a tangled web and could not get out. I remember talking to God in the best way I knew how, saying, "Lord, you gotta help me out."

It was not until one final incident put those I loved most in danger that I finally woke up. This incident involved my friends Devon and Will. Will and I went to Fox Hill Mall. Devon paged me, "Man, I got this guy from out of town. He wants to get a half a key." All I was thinking about was money because half a key went for $21,000.

Immediately I called my brother. I told him I needed half a key – we used to call it a "bird."

I confirmed with Devon I could make the deal and arranged for it to go down at my mother's house. I was so caught up in making the money I did not think about the danger I could be putting my mom in. So, my brother brought the shipment over.

Will and I waited at the house for Devon and his buyer to come. Mom was in the other room. At first, he was hesitant to come in, but I convinced him that everything was safe. I had about $8,000.00 in my socks.

When the buyer came in, he quickly shifted tones and yelled, "Where is the stuff?" holding a gun straight at us.

"Man, what's going on?"

"Just tell me where the stuff is!"

I said, "Man, the stuff is right here." The guy said, "If your mama comes out, I'm going to blow her head off." When he said that, my mind was saying, "Don't move. Don't move. Don't move."

At that moment, I made up my mind. If my mother came through that door, I was going to have to rush him. He demanded I give him the stuff. I showed him where it was. He took it and spun off in his car down the street.

Then I ran down the street to Will's house and we jumped in the car to go find the guy. We could not find him and so we went back to my house. When we got there, a buddy named Harlan and Devon were both in front of my house. Devon was in the car on the passenger side and the driver's side window was open. I dove through the window and began to beat him up. "You set me up!" I kept saying with every hit.

A couple of days after that, word on the street was that Devon himself said he set me up. Then I saw him at our burrito shop off Vernon and Hooper. I reached down under my seat, and he saw me and took off.

A week later I was with my girlfriend at my mom's house. I got a call from someone, telling me that Devon was at my friend Declan's house. Sharon said, "Don't go around there." But I took her Toyota and drove off, and there were Declan and Devon, walking across the street. There was a car in front of Declan's house.

As they were coming close to me, I began to confront him, saying, "So you are telling people you set me up, huh?"

He responded, "Man, what are you talking about?"

When I got closer to him, I swung at him. He spun around, reached in his belt and pulled a gun out. He was aiming the gun straight at me, but Will grabbed him, and I took off running.

That was the experience that finally made me determined to leave the life. Years later, I called Will to see how things were in the neighborhood. We went to the Fox Hill Mall like we used to. We were riding and talking and asking how everyone was doing, and he caught me up with all the happenings.

As soon as we arrived at the mall and got out of the car, who was there standing before me? It was Devon!

The emotions began to rise in me; the feelings in the pit of my stomach started moving – reflections of the danger he put my mother in; his betrayal, then his back-stabbing and attempt to shoot me.

When we locked eyes, he was surprised too. I felt like I was in slow motion when I began to step toward him, with all the tension flooding my body.

Then we spoke to one another very casually. When I got closer to him, I reached out and grabbed him, and pulled him in. I spoke to him and said, "Thank you." Of course, he did not know what I was thanking him for! I was thanking him because his evil actions against me were the thing that made me make the final decision to get out of the life. What he meant for my evil, God used for my good.

Telling the Neighborhood Goodbye

Even after I decided to leave the life, I had a proclivity to go "backward" to places I used to frequent, knowing deep down that I needed to just make a clean slate and not look back. It was hard!

I was driving one day and wanted to go check on my buddy, Randy. As I drove by his mechanic shop, I heard a voice telling me, "Just wave and keep going; don't stop, keep going."

A few hours later, one of my friends called me and told me that Randy and his brother were surprised by some police imposters. Randy had gone up the street and his brother stayed in the shop. These fake cops handcuffed his brother, and when

Randy came running down the street to see what was going on, they handcuffed him too and shot them both execution-style twice in the head. I immediately reflected on the voice that told me to wave and keep going. I could have been there at the same time, but God was watching out for me. I felt His presence and was thankful that I obeyed his voice. That was the last time I went in that neighborhood.

CHAPTER 17

Trouble at Home

DAVID: Well, Sharon and I were going through a rough time in our marriage. We both were imperfect. Lord knows I had my many issues. But then, I found out she was cheating on me and that really did something to my ego and my pride. I took that very hard.

Here I was selling drugs, living the fast life, and providing for my family -- maybe not being the most attentive mate, but my family wanted for nothing. I was bringing the green paper home! But as I began to realize I needed to leave that life, I also realized that perhaps my priorities needed to shift.

1996 Separation Time

The day came that I wish on no man, no husband, and no father. I was in the kitchen washing dishes when my wife came in and said, "You have to leave. I want you out of here now!" Sadly, the children overheard our discourses. By then we had six children - two of whom were babies.

My daughter was more in tune with the fact that her mommy and daddy were not getting along. It hurt her so bad she began to rub my hand and look at me, as if to say, "It's okay Daddy, it's okay." She kept rubbing my hand to comfort me as I was crying, not wanting to lose my family.

My wife was saying, "I love you, but I am not in love with you anymore." At first, I said, "I'm not going anywhere– it's my house also." The police finally arrived to talk with me about my rights and left it to me to decide whether to stay or go. After all, I was right - it was my house too. My sisters arrived too, and they encouraged me to go. The children did not need to see the tension, and as much as I did not want to,

> We did not have
> a healthy relationship,
> and her wanting out
> was the best thing
> she ever did;
> she left me with me.

I eventually decided it was best to go ahead and leave.

I will never forget the look on my daughter's face and those big eyes saying, "I love you, Daddy." Both of my daughters were so precious to me. My boys were also my joy, and I wanted to be with them to help raise them. This was my nightmare.

Inside I was reflecting on our journey before we got married until we decided we wanted to marry. I remembered how I cheated on her, and now it felt like I was reaping what I had sowed. It felt like payback, and it was all my fault. If I had sowed good seeds into my relationship, I thought, perhaps we would not be going through this.

We were together for thirteen years. For many years, she was the "fall guy" to my rage and my outbursts. I would take it out on her. She would push my triggers when she would question me about other women. I was guilty but I felt she did not have the right to question me, and it made me feel guilty the way she would ask me. I would slap her and tell her she did not know what she was talking about. I was abusive in every sense of the word: emotionally, physically, and psychologically. Sharon didn't realize she married a "rageoholic." She bore the brunt of my rage. I didn't deserve her; she definitely did not deserve how I treated her. We did not have a healthy relationship, and her wanting out was the best thing she ever did; she left me with me. I did not want to leave my children, but I needed help that I was not getting.

There was also so much I had overlooked over time as it related to her cheating on me. Our breakup did not happen overnight: the children had told me at times when another man had come by and gone into her room. I had hoped the more I showed her how faithful I was now, that she would not need to go outside of our marriage, but the damage had already been done and the consequences were manifesting. I thought about how I had hurt her.

My sisters arrived right on time to help me move out from her house and they took me to church that evening. I did not want to go. I was hurting so much, that I did not know what I wanted.

I sat as far in the back as I could away from people. But no matter how far away I sat, the Pastor still found me. The guest speaker zeroed in on me and began to speak to me and tell me what God wanted to do in my life.

Offering Time

As I passed by the guest speaker, he said, "Stop, stop everything, this man is a prophet and I have to lay my hands on him." He looked at me and said, "Brother, I am going to lay my hands on you." All I remember is I went out, and I heard my sisters screaming. In reflecting on that moment, it felt like God had been waiting and waiting for me to surrender. I just cried like a baby on the ground.

When the man prophesied to me, he spoke things about my past that only God could have told him, and he also spoke things of my future that I could not even see. It was powerful. He declared I would preach - and not only just preach, but I would be a powerful preacher. This was contradictory to anything I wanted to do; I would tell my sisters they were crazy when they would speak into my life, but this night was the night of my reckoning with God.

God told me "You gotta let it go" through one of the prophets I came across. I kept trying to fix my broken marriage and regain my family. The prophet said, "You have to let it go all the way." It was hard because I kept blaming myself for the whole breakup. I wanted my family back! It was destroying me from the inside out.

After church, I went straight to my mother's house. From there, I ended up attending Abundance of Christ under the leadership of Apostle Richard Harris. I went back to my family the next day and Sharon was saying she wanted to move to Compton. I offered to help her move. I realized I had to let her live her life.

CHAPTER 18

I Couldn't Walk Away

PASTOR CK: How did you meet your next wife? Was it smooth sailing in the beginning?

DAVID: After Sharon and I broke up, I was in church trying to keep myself holy. I needed healing, but instead, I stuffed my feelings so that I did not have to deal with them. I was trying to keep myself by myself before we got married, by sheer willpower. By this time, I was also leading worship at our church. But I was so broken. I had not dealt with all my issues. I tried to keep myself pure, but it did not work.

I received a phone call one day from a lady who was part of my church named Michelle. "How did you get my number?" I asked.

"One of your sisters gave it to me," she giggled. "I hope you don't mind me calling you."

After this, we would talk to one another almost every day. I must admit, it was a welcomed distraction from all that I was going through with Sharon. I looked forward to speaking with Michelle. She was from Belize, and I had never met a woman from another country.

PASTOR CK: So, what did your mother think of Michelle?

DAVID: At first it was ok with Mom. Until one day Michelle and I got into an argument. My mother was in the room and my auntie was visiting from out of town. Michelle and I were arguing, and she was trying to hit me; before I knew it she ran into the kitchen, grabbed a knife, and came after me; but my mother went after her and grabbed her. My mother yelled at me, "Don't you ever turn your back on a woman like this. I don't want this woman in my house." Michelle left upset, but she knew my mother meant business.

My mother told my pastor and they prayed for me to walk in wisdom. But I was so intoxicated by the relationship that when she called me we started talking with one another again and I disregarded everything we went through. Our flesh got the best of us.

I did not tell my pastor I was talking to her or seeing her. Over time, he got wind of me seeing her and decided to give me some food for thought. He said, "Son, she is the type of woman that is a Christian every now and then."

He was trying to give me enough information for me to make a wise decision. Finally, I confessed I had slept with her to my pastor. He asked me what I was going to do and gave me an ultimatum: Either get married, stop seeing her, or step down in ministry.

He would not allow a fornicator to be over his people. The ball was in my court, and I wanted to do the right and honorable thing before God. I was willing to do whatever I needed to do to make things right, but my weak flesh made the wrong decision and married her.

PASTOR CK: So, did you have counseling before marriage?

DAVID: No. While we were doing a brief counseling session with my pastor right before the wedding, he said, "I wish you would have come to me before you decided to marry this woman." He said that my wife was broken and that I was broken, and the two pieces did not fit together at all.

PASTOR CK: You couldn't walk away?

DAVID: I was pressed to do the right thing. I had been with her, slept with her, and the right thing in my mind was to make it right. I wish I had the wisdom and the courage to walk away based on what I know now.

PASTOR CK: Hindsight is 20/20, David. Your pastor was on the right track, but you needed some deeper counseling. Coming from such an abusive background as you did, you were not ready to be in a healthy relationship.

You have done a lot of forgiving and letting go. I hope that is an ongoing process when you look at your life through the lens of Christ's Grace.

DAVID: I agree. God restrained me as I was walking through this marriage.

The day before the marriage, my brother overheard us arguing and he came to me and asked, "Man, are you sure? This ain't right, take your time man if this ain't it." I didn't want to hear it; I was so blinded by my love and my commitment to do the right thing. I ignored all the red flags.

The funny thing is, my mom could see that she was not the one before we married and she asked me, "Are you sure you want to get married to this woman?" She later told me that, before we married, all the signs were saying, "STOP!!!!"

Michelle didn't like my mom and she shouted at me one day as we argued, "I wish your mother would die!!!!" I had just come home from the hospital from seeing my mom and that cut me like a knife. I couldn't believe the evil that this woman just spewed out of her mouth. She knew that my mother was dying of stage 4 cancer. How could she make such a diabolical statement? All I could do was weep.

On the day of our wedding, I knew my mom wanted me to be happy. If she had her way, I would not be marrying Michelle; but because she loved me, she did not stand in my way. She would say softly, "Son, are you sure?" She was present at the wedding as frail as she was; she was determined to see her youngest son get married.

The wedding was relatively nice, and everything ended up as planned. About a week later, we moved into an apartment together.

I did not know how dramatic jealousy could get in a marriage, but I soon found out. She grew more insanely jealous. The things that came out of her mouth at times were pure evil. I could be singing a song, and some lady would be listening intently to me, and she would accuse me of having an affair with her. She would look around the room and spot women who were enjoying my singing and attach the women to me.

One time we were at church to celebrate the release of a new CD, and as the event began, I walked up to the stage, and the church was packed with the saints. My wife was in the first row where she could see everything.

The anointing of the Lord was tangibly present, but as soon as I sat down, she was in my ear with negativity, accusing me of singing not to the Lord but to this under-aged girl. Her insane jealousy broke my spirit that night. I just wished she had more self-esteem than she had. That whole night we argued, going back and forth over this senselessness. I could not convince her that I was faithful only to her. Instead of her celebrating with me about my brand-new CD, she was overtaken by the spirit of jealousy and thought my success would take me away from her.

One day, I left due to Michelle's arguing. I went to stay in my mom's apartment. I went to see my mom first, and she said, "Y'all just got married. I told you not to be with that woman, but you want to do your own thing." My brother's wife said, "Y'all can get an annulment, you know." I just shook my head because I was at a loss. I did what I thought was pleasing to God and the right thing, and it was frustrating to see it go so badly every day.

I felt so lonely and sad in this relationship. I felt empty with no real love in my life, and so alone as I had chosen a woman who did not know how to give or receive love. I believed my children loved me, but this woman whom I called my wife was far from it. I could see it more clearly now after so much emotional debris was gone. I was able to see my situation just as it was: a big mistake.

One day while driving to a service, we were bitterly arguing, and the background singers in the car with us called us on the carpet. We had been married by now just two years. It seemed to never stop. It was always something, and when we were not arguing, she was leaving out of the blue with her two boys and staying away for hours.

One time my daughter spent the night and my wife and I got into an argument. My daughter said, "Daddy, I don't like this woman, she is mean." Seeing my child's face as she said this, I knew I had to do something. I began to pray in earnest for the leading of the Lord.

I remember one time, as I was preparing for the word, she began to demean me. We made it to church, and she sat in the front row as usual. All the time I was preaching the word, she sat there, her head cocked to the left with a "gangster lean" as if to say, "Boy, please, you ain't saying nothing." She had no respect for the word, the church, or me. She accused me of seeing one of the ladies in the group. We were having a revival and after the service, Pastor asked me what was going on with us.

My wife showed partiality when my kids came over. My kids complained all the time about her open hostility towards them. Whatever her kids told her about mine, she believed. She left me a couple of times and would come back when she wanted to. Things went from worse to worst!

This was an unbelievable marriage. I must admit that I was harsh in my judgment of her. I would talk about her badly as well. It was incredibly challenging - and then God would convict me. I felt ashamed about how I was acting, and I would repent, but she continued to hurt me. I prayed and eventually, God helped me to grow to the point where I kept my mouth shut and I was able to use restraint and never hit her. But oh - how I wanted to.

One time out of the blue she slapped me, and I turned my face and cried, I was so mad. I wanted to sock her. She would scandalize my name in conversation with whoever would listen. She would talk about me and say how dumb I was, how I couldn't even read or write well, and how I should be thankful to be with her. Marriage to her was hard! We argued about everything: bacon, detergent, what to watch on TV.

The last time she left, I came home to an empty house with only wooden crates to sit on. The landlord came by my house and told me I had to leave. I advised him that the rent was paid, but he still said that I had thirty days to vacate the premises. Because the house had been rented in my sister's name, there was nothing else I could do. The Lord ministered to me and let me know that in 30 days I would have somewhere else to go. I immediately felt my faith rise.

A New Start

Thirty days later, God's word came to pass. I received a call from a landlord in Norwalk to rent one of the rooms in her home. Not only did I have a place to go, but God gave me my deposit back from the first and last payment I put down. God was showing me so much favor I cried in gratitude and worship. At this place, I was able to save my money and have some peace of mind. It allowed me the intimacy that I needed to grow closer to God with no relationships distracting me.

One day, Michelle called me. I nervously answered the phone because I wanted to rekindle the relationship and honor God's word about marriage. She sounded a little different, which gave me hope.

She wanted to see me, so she met me out in front of the house, and we sat in the car for hours. We apologized to each other, forgave each other, and decided to give our marriage another chance. We agreed that this would please God. We talked for weeks and kept in touch.

My brother called me one day and said I could come rent a room from him if I wanted to. I felt loved and thankful that he wanted me to rent from him, plus it was closer to my job. I gave my landlord a 30-day notice and she respected my decision to go.

Michelle had a place on West Blvd when I moved to his house. My friend drove me over to Michelle's house. When we drove up, Michelle jumped out of the car, and my friend saw that she was sitting kind of close to the man that was in the car. I shrugged it off and ignored his comments.

She called me one day to tell me that they were having a party for her son. I said, "OK, I will get my twins and come to the party." The party started about 5 pm, and the boys and I walked in, and a lot of people were there. My sons went directly to her son to start playing with him. I was sitting on the couch relaxing, while her Belizean friends were drinking; it was my first time seeing her drink.

My sons came to me and said "Daddy, I didn't know she drank and cussed like that." I got my kids and told her we were going to leave; she responded, "I'm about to get some rest too." Her girlfriend busted her by asking, "Aren't we going to the party?" She shut them down by interrupting them. I heard them but just kept going out the door.

Michelle Loses Her Apartment

I received an urgent call from Michelle one morning and she was upset. I tried to calm her down so she could tell me what was going on. "I don't have anywhere to stay," she said. I responded, "What happened Michelle?" "I just got to go," she said.

I said, "Well, I'm going to have to talk to my brother because this is not my place, and plus, it's really small." I wanted to try to make my marriage work - I did not want it to fail, and perhaps this was an opportunity to get back together. I spoke with my brother, and he opened his heart and his doors to Michelle and her children. They moved in by the next week.

But soon, I noticed a pattern develop: every Friday Michelle would tell me that she was about to go to her sister's house for a while, and then I would not see her until Monday. I could not believe what I was seeing: she would just ghost me and leave with her kids until she decided to come back to the house.

The Arguments Return

We said we would not argue anymore when we were talking and trying to get back together, but over time the same patterns began to resurface. She continued to disappear and did not return for several days.

I was taking Michelle to work one morning, and she lit in on me about the kids. She didn't like me disciplining her kids - it would send her over the hill. While I was driving on the 105, the boys were playing in the back and were too loud. "Pipe down boys," I said. Michelle got angry and began to go off on me for telling her boys to be quiet. She began to call me all sorts of things, and my blood began to boil. All I could do was talk to God while this woman was disrespecting me. I knew God kept me, but I accelerated in speed, and I responded to her, and my firmness came out. She got quiet. Once we dropped the kids off at their dad's house, we were alone, and she started back up. Man, I wanted to leave and never come back.

My heart desired to see this marriage through and to go through the "richer or poorer, sickness and in health, until death do us part"; through the ups and the downs; through likes, love, and "can't stand you" moments. But she was stuck on being single one day and married another day. I just could not live like that. That was not a covenant marriage, and I communicated to her that she needed to be faithful to her vows, to me and the Lord. She ignored me.

Children see the truth. My son told me that my wife would constantly show favoritism to her sons over my kids when I was not around. I remember the day that I had to let her go. I knew that God wanted something different for me and my children. I waited until she got home to talk with her. She denied everything. We argued but I was convinced my children were not lying. "You and your kids have to go," I said. After that God said, "I want you to detach yourself from this toxic relationship and let me show you what I want you to have."

Shortly afterward, she took off and was gone for a week. She tried to come back, but this time I heard the Lord and I listened to Him. God said, "She is not going where you are going; do not take her back." So, I let her go. I advised her that she and her kids had to leave. She was talking crazy and blaming me for the breakup. She filed for divorce. When I got the papers, I was one happy man. I could hardly believe it!

My sister prophesied to me after this very broken relationship. She said, "Do not move on your own understanding again. Allow God to take the lead. He is going to get you out of this." I felt God affirm that word to me.

Soon after she prophesied that, the divorce papers came through the mail. I happily signed them.

God had truly released me. Yet my wife continued her smear campaign against me. She ruined my credit. She went to a friend's house telling them that I had given her a disease and tried to ruin my reputation.

Marriage to her was hard! I must admit that when it came to choosing a mate, until I surrendered that part of my life to Christ, I was blinded by my brokenness. I picked women for the wrong reasons and stayed with them for the wrong reasons also.

After Michelle, I cried out to the Lord for him to help me be the man that my pastor said I could be if I just submitted my body and mortified my flesh; I wanted to walk as that holy man. He was my role model and the one I respected highly. I made up my mind: this time, I was going all the way with Jesus. I determined I was going to wait until Jesus sent me my queen.

PASTOR CK: So you found that peace and discipline in Christ.

DAVID: Yes, I did. Through prayer, accountability, worshiping, and singing, God kept me.

It was powerful because I had Apostle Richard Harris as my role model. He was a single man, and he would always tell me that it was possible for me to live a holy life. He was my visual, as he modeled the fact that it could be done and showed me how.

Once I got under Apostle Harris' leadership, he began to mentor me and teach me. He taught me how to be a man. It was a good model, because I have never seen that man go through any type of scandal. He never showed me any indication. He always said you got to live right before the people.

I began my new journey and it felt good. But I had a lot to learn because there were many women in his church and the more I sang, the more they gravitated my way. I had a lot of new lessons coming my way in the church context, but for now, God had me in his house.

CHAPTER 19

A New Dream

DAVID: As an adult, I was always guarding against being abandoned. In times past, I had walls to protect me–walls of anger and rage, walls of fear and insecurities.

Having been abandoned, I never felt good enough, never felt like anyone would want to stay with me. My mom spent such little time with me that as an adult, when my wife or whoever I was with spent time somewhere other than with me, I felt jealous and afraid that they were going to leave me eventually.

> Thank God,
> now I know that I can
> expose those thoughts,
> and when I talk about
> them, they either vanish
> or calm down.

PASTOR CK: Now, how do you navigate or process the trauma relating to intimate relationships and the fear of being left?

DAVID: Today I can articulate my feelings and talk about them. I can verbalize what it means to me. In times past, I always had the fear of being left by my previous wives and usually would internalize it. I would go on the attack out of fear of being abandoned. Thank God, now I know that I can expose those thoughts, and when I talk about them, they either vanish or calm down. Thank God that now I have a wife that I can trust and who trusts me. I have a wife that is willing to walk with me through my healing. I have been truly blessed!

The closer I grow to Christ, the more I understand what happened to me. It was like what Job 3:25b said, "For the thing I greatly feared has come upon me." Once bad things started to happen, I lived in constant fear of being less than and being left behind. I expected the worst, and so it was. Abandonment, I understood, could disguise itself in many forms... from a mother not being there, my wives leaving me, and even some of my children wanting nothing to do with me.

Today when I feel detached from someone I love, I must verbalize my feelings. I must name it and insist on a conversation. Communication is important. I can still respect people and today I can verbalize the need for attention without anger.

PASTOR CK: David, you have shared an enormous amount of your journey. Thank you. Every reader who picks up your book will clearly see the protection and mercies of God in your life. Can you share why it was important to tell this portion of your story?

DAVID: I am convinced that God has a greater purpose for me - and not only me, but many other young boys, teenagers, our adult men who were raised in broken situations. Our brokenness shapes us into the boys and men we become, but Jesus makes all the difference.

PASTOR CK: I agree. And when you live to talk about it, it makes it apparent that God has greater plans for you despite the rejection, abuse, and abandonment. What would you say has been valuable about our process?

DAVID: First, you believe in my story and that is huge for me. I needed a safe space to talk, reflect, cry, ask for forgiveness, and also forgive others. You gave me that space to do so. You always say, "People are sick as their secrets." I do not want any secrets in my life making me sick or sicker.

PASTOR CK: I commend you, David, for your courage and for your humility to tell your story. How do you want to conclude this part of your journey?

DAVID: Well, this is Part One of my journey. We will work on the sequel in 2025. But there are a few more accounts that I want to share that impacted my life and were instrumental in turning me in the right direction.

Music Found Me

After I stopped dealing drugs and began to lay low, I found myself humming music more and more. At first, I did not think anything of it. I do not know if I had the blues because of the drama inside and outside of my home.

When I finally stopped selling drugs and walked away from that fast and dangerous lifestyle, I used to lock myself up in my closet and practice singing every day. One day I found myself going over an old buddy's house from the neighborhood where we all grew up. I knew he had a studio in the back of his house, but because of the life I lived, it never interested me until now.

His father was a famous musician who was part of a singing group called the Chamberlain Brothers. On that day, my buddy was just playing, and I started singing. He looked up and said, "Hey, I didn't know you could sing like that, man." He was shocked. I was singing along with him playing a song called "Loving You." It was the first time I heard myself in a studio.

He taped me in the studio and gave me a copy of the recording. After I listened to it, I was shocked and proud at the same time. I didn't think my voice had star quality, but that's what he told me. I began to let other people listen to it. I would get a lot of compliments which made me feel good and appreciated. Music is strange like that.

I had found a new passion. I kept on practicing and over time I was getting accustomed to hearing my voice. I started having dreams and aspirations about big concerts. I saw myself on stage like a big singing star. I wanted it; I craved it.

The guys at the studio had a men's group. They were encouraging - they liked my sound and supported me in getting my first demo, which was the song "Inseparable." From there I looked in the newspaper and found a man named Shane. He was in Hollywood, and I hired him as a producer. We did a rough demo, and then I had to rent a studio in Hollywood. One day, somebody told me that West Angeles was having a talent show at their church. I felt it was time for me to enter the contest. I told Shane I needed a track; he asked what I wanted to sing, and I said, "God Bless the Child." Shane did a track and so I entered the talent show at West Angeles. It was my first time on stage experiencing this kind of presentation.

I invited my mom and family. The night came and it was truly happy. My mom was pleased. She cheered me on, and my brothers and sisters were so proud. I began to sing, and the audience responded so favorably: I won second place.

After this, I wrote my first song, "Baby, I Be Good to You." Shane helped me hire background singers and we cut our song.

I was proud and I wanted everyone to hear it, including my kids and Sharon. Sharon gave my demo to one of her friends at her job, who then gave the demo to one of her producer friends. The next thing I knew, I got a call to set up an appointment with them.

A New Dream

At first, I wanted to do a solo album. Then, a couple of people wanted me to join their band and call the group PHAZE 3, so I agreed to. They were getting ready to do a record with a record company.

The band was cool, and it was nice being with some brothers who had experience and exposure to the singing industry. I learned how to sing in harmony. The four of us started performing at clubs and getting a serious buzz. Some of those performances turned into concerts.

One night a manager saw us singing somewhere. He told us, "I wanted to sign you guys as soon as I heard you." Then there was this alternative group that was on the Arsenio Hall Show. They got us connected with some leads in Hollywood. Most of our performances now were in the Hollywood neighborhood, where all the white folk were partying. They loved our harmony, and soon we were doing private parties for millionaires.

I remember singing for Vidal Sassoon's event. Boy, that was wild. The crowd, the women, and everything that came with it was there. We ended up being invited to the Vidal Building because he wanted to hear our singing more. He had some executives present and some of the people that we met at the party.

Our group was known for soulful singing, and I was known as one who stood out from the group. I would hit this long note at the end and hold it and they would go crazy.

We did not get signed through Vidal or his executives, but the buzz continued to bring us to Hollywood, and we began to have our own following. I remember meeting Michael Concepcion's representative. He was the one who produced MC Hammer and notable entertainers like All in the Same Gang. But the connections would only go so far each time.

I was not going for it; it was all of us or none of us.

In the end, we were finally signed, but we did not pay enough attention to the contracts. Looking back, that was our downfall just as it was for many young groups.

Tension in the Signing Selection

We also noticed a trend happening every time we were considered to be signed. They wanted to sign me and have the rest of the group as supporters to me. I did not like that, but it slowly drew a wedge between us. Because my voice stood out the most, the producers would gravitate to me.

We went to Electric Records and Motown Records, and each time they didn't want to sign the group – they wanted to sign me. Finally, we went to Quest Records. Boy, were we excited! You would have thought we won the California Lottery.

We nailed the audition. But in the back room, the same old same old would emerge -- they only wanted to sign me, and the rest of the group could serve as my background singers. This was so discouraging to us as a group, and it felt so divisive. I was not going for it; it was all of us or none of us. Yet as much as I stood on that principle and tried to show the group how dedicated I was to them, it still caused jealousy and a divide.

Eventually, it was not only a divide there, but even at home with my children's mother, Sharon. I would turn down the deals offered to me, and she and others would be like, "What's wrong with you?" They did not understand. It was my commitment to my group. I did not believe in going alone after all they did for me and all we experienced together.

After a while, I said to the group, "Man, you know, if I get signed, I will definitely fight for you all. But let's get in the door at least, how about that for now?"

In 1993, our group did a compilation album with other artists. On it, we did a remake of "It Takes a Fool". RCA Records heard it and came to me, and said they wanted just me as a solo artist. I turned it down because they did not want my group. My manager said, "If they didn't want the group, just put 'David B and PHAZE 3.'" But the group said, "No way!" It began to be clear that we had some challenges ahead of us.

Summer Jam 1994-1995

We were the first group that did the national anthem at Irvine Meadows. We connected with John London and The Beat 92.3. We ended up doing the national anthem at the Summer Jam two years straight.

We opened for Usher, and many singing entertainers were there like Jodeci. We were being asked to give our autographs. We were blown away by the gravitation of the crowds. We had never experienced that before.

Looking back, I truly thank God that I did not get caught up with that lifestyle. If you do not know what you are doing it can be very dangerous. In fact, this was the point where our group finally broke up.

Practicing My New Craft

I found myself mimicking different singers, like Luther Vandross, Teddy Pendergrass, Al Green, and Patti Labelle. I taped myself with a regular tape recorder, so I could hear myself.

One day, it finally came: the opportunity of a lifetime to sign with a solid record company. RCA was the hot place to be signed with.

I heard a voice inside my head ask me, "Do you want something temporal or eternal?" Somehow, I knew it was God leading me to not go that way anymore.

After I heard God's voice, I went to my manager and told him I could not do it. The manager said, "You got to be kidding, here is an opportunity to change your whole life." I jumped in my car and that was the last of that. And even though I had arrived at this destination, something deep within me was not at peace. In hindsight, I have to say sometimes you can chase a particular dream for a long time, and once you get it, it doesn't have the depth or weight you thought it would. I felt a pulling away from my R&B roots and a commission to my new life in Christ, to use my gifts for the glory of God.

Even though I was being compelled to go in a different direction, part of me just didn't want to sing anymore. I felt that singing R&B contributed to my bad luck. Then, one day, I was at a men's prayer breakfast. I was just sitting there, and they had praise and worship, and this man was singing. I got lost in the music and began to sing, and my voice stood out. The guy in charge looked at me and invited me forward and I started singing the hook. The men started going crazy. They were shocked! I told them, "I was in a men's band."

Every time I was singing in front of the people, it was like heat coming through my belly. It was just like a burning sensation.

CHAPTER 20

Redemption

DAVID: One morning, as I was praying to the Lord and worshipping, I heard God say to me "I am about to take your mom." I lost it!!! It was so emotional, I yelled back at God, "No! Why now? We are just getting back together again." I did not understand why he would do this to us.

A week later my brother and his wife brought Mom home from a doctor's appointment and they sat me down to tell me that Mom was diagnosed with stage four colon cancer. They told Mom they needed to operate on her to stop the spread.

I was devastated. I fell to my knees and started praying and crying, "You allowed me to rekindle my relationship and now you are going to take her away from me!"

Day of the Surgery

Before this diagnosis, I always considered my mom to be strong and fearless - until she looked up at me before they rolled her into the operating room and said, "Son, I'm afraid." I took my mother's hand and began to pray for her. Tears rolled down her face as I let her know I would be right there when she came out.

We learned after they opened my mom up that the cancer had spread all over her body. I was devastated. My mom began to decline fast. She also began to do chemo. One day when she wanted to go to church, she was sitting where the mother's board sat. The power of God hit her, and she jumped up and began to dance before the Lord. The music had stopped, but my mom kept going as if God had given her a revelation – she was frail, but the strength of the Lord was dancing within her. At that moment, I saw my mom in a whole different light. After that night, she had a whole different disposition. She was not afraid anymore.

I would always go see my mom and pray with her after work, but she declined every time I saw her. One day my siblings had to take her to the hospital. After I got off work, I and my family went to see her. It was so hard for me, that at first, I could not go in the room with Michelle and the children.

The last time I visited her in her room, my heart was beating fast. I was nervous - my stomach was upset, and my emotions were all over the place. It broke my heart to see my mother in this situation. I was in a pain that I could not even describe. I remember being at work as a security guard, and throughout the day, I was feeling the anticipatory grief of knowing I was losing her. My home life did not make it better, and I felt like my support and my rock was leaving me.

Those days of spending time with her and the opportunity to live with her taught me a different side of her; I learned to love her and be her son and let her be my mom. We got close to each other in a way that I didn't think was ever possible after all we had been through. All my resentment and anger toward her for her abandoning me was gone. God empowered us both to love one another the way it was always supposed to be during that time.

As I journeyed with her through her last days, she would whisper, "The Father, the Son, and the Holy Ghost" when she was in her greatest pain. In response, I would say, "Fight, Mom!"

I remember her last day. When I left that morning, I felt like something was about to take place. God woke me up and I prayed and prayed, crying out to him; my eyes were swollen red and watery.

When I arrived at work it was only me and another guy on shift. All of a sudden, I got a call from my brother Larry. He said, "Momma is no longer responding now."

She was sitting up on the couch watching a soap opera in her favorite chair. When he told me, I told my job, "I have to go; it's my mother." I jumped in my car and took off to his place.

When I opened the door, she was sitting there. I yelled, "Mom." She opened her eyes, said, "We okay," and closed her eyes again. Larry came and picked her up and carried her to her bed as she continued to rest.

Michelle was there already. We eventually went home. Larry said, "She's not gone yet."

Around 3 am, the phone rang, and Larry said, "She's gone." We came back and I knelt by her and said, "I'm proud of you...Momma I'm proud of you."

God said, "You have to release her, David."

Preparing for the Funeral

My sister-in-law Denise put a beautiful funeral together for us siblings. She called her sister from Chicago who came out; her ex-husband also came out. My pastor Apostle Richard Harris did the Eulogy, and he provided an emotional Spirit-filled service honoring my mother. He loved her so much, and you could tell by the way he handled the service from beginning to end.

We were all on the first row never wanting to see this day, but here we were honoring our mom. I had the tall task of singing at her funeral, which I was not sure if I could get through. But the strength of God empowered me to sing in honor of my mom. After I sang, tears flowed like a river from the depths of my soul.

Apostle Richard Harris' Eulogy was personal. "I remember when I would have David in the back at the ministerial meeting," he said, "and his mother would always send someone to the back and say, 'Tell pastor to tell David I am ready to go home.' That's what she told God: 'I'm ready to go home.'"

When we left for the burial place to commit her body back to the ground, I felt numb through that whole process, as if we were going in slow motion. When they dropped her body in the ground and covered it with the dirt until it was full, I knew I could never talk to her again; I could never have 3 am prayer with her anymore – this was it; this was final; and it broke me into pieces like a little baby. I felt lost; I felt part of me went into that grave with my momma. I did not know what would happen after this; I did not know how I would live my life after this day without her - only God knew.

> I did not want her to go, but the peace of God was tangibly present with me during that season.

I had my family, my praying sisters, and my pastor, who was always available for me whenever I needed to talk to him. But I was numb for a long time, and I spent more time in my kitchen prayer closet every time I needed to talk to God, crying before Him and lamenting through my grief. Her death drew me closer to God every single day.

I thank God that he restored my relationship with my mom, and we were able to enjoy each other before she died. I cannot explain it, but I felt spiritually free when she passed away. I did not want her to go, but the peace of God was tangibly present with me during that season.

I felt free of all the baggage I had carried from childhood. I felt free to enjoy the memories we had created as adults before she passed. I did not have to hold the pain of my past against her.

What a great feeling. It was hard losing her, but peaceful and freeing at the same time.

PASTOR CK: What has this process of counseling and writing your book been like to you?

DAVID: I have never been so vulnerable in my life. Answering all your probing questions allowed me to bring up the truth, facts, and areas that I needed to forgive and let go. It was shocking and unpredictable concerning my emotions. There were things I thought were resolved, but this process revealed the work continues inside of me. I am deeply appreciative and forever thankful. You said this writing process would bring healing to my life; I did not see it all at first; but I can say I am on a healing journey. Thank you for being my pastor, my mentor, my spiritual mom, and a safe friend in this whole process.

To God be the glory! I have found my queen, and I found her in church. Never have I been so totally accepted by anyone. She loves me with all my warts and all my scars. She loves me unconditionally and this is something that I have never experienced before in any kind of relationship. I still have a way to grow, but I am grateful for the queen that the Lord has seen fit to put in my life. I have never had a love that has lasted this long. We have been married for over 14 years and I have enjoyed experiences that I had previously only seen in the movies. We enjoy true friendship. My next book will be devoted to true love! Marriage for me, the third time around, has been a joyous ride!

ABOUT THE AUTHOR

David B. Nellum is a native of Los Angeles, CA. He accepted Christ as a young man and accepted his call to preach in his early 30's. He was ordained an Evangelist under the Ministry of Apostle Robbie Horton as a young man. David has four beautiful adult children from his first marriage, and is the proud grandfather of six grandchildren.

Today, Evangelist David serves faithfully at his home church, Acts Community Bible Church, under the Leadership and Pastorate of Rev. Dr. Candace Kelly, where he serves in many areas of leadership: teaching, preaching, prayer ministry, and serving on the praise team.

Gifted in many ways, Evangelist David has a passion for music, radio/tv broadcasting, and the arts. He has been part of two male singing groups (PHAZE 3 and DDT) and has been signed by prominent recording labels. David has also performed in Gospel musical dramas. He is currently working on his new Gospel single, "A Sound from Heaven", to be released in the summer of 2024.

Under his successful ministry, Stillness in His Presence Ministries, he hosts a weekly broadcast entitled Breaking the Cycle, which airs on The Power of Praise Network. He also hosts a weekly Facebook Live prayer ministry of encouragement every Sunday evening at 5:00pm (Pacific Standard Time). Evangelist David lives in Lakewood, California and has been married to his lovely wife Diane Nellum for 14 years.

Contact Information:

For Booking and Speaking Engagements, please contact Evangelist David Nellum at the following:

Email: sihpministries@gmail.com